D1037351

How to
Find Hidden
Real Estate
Bargains

OTHER McGRAW-HILL BOOKS BY ROBERT IRWIN

Handbook of Property Management

Computerizing Your Real Estate Office

The McGraw-Hill Real Estate Handbook

Mingles: A Home Buying Guide for Unmarried Couples (paperback)

Timeshare Properties: What Every Buyer *Must* Know!

The New Mortgage Game

Protect Yourself in Real Estate: The Complete Beginner's Guide (paperback)

The Real Estate Agent's and Investor's Tax Book (with Richard Brickman)

How to Buy a Home at a Reasonable Price (paperback)

How to Buy and Sell Real Estate for Financial Security (paperback)

ROBERT IRWIN

How to Find Hidden Real Estate Bargains

McGraw-Hill Book Company
New York   St. Louis   San Francisco   Auckland   Bogotá
Hamburg   Johannesburg   London   Madrid
Mexico   Montreal   New Delhi   Panama
Paris   São Paulo   Singapore
Sydney   Tokyo   Toronto

Library of Congress Cataloging-in-Publication Data

Irwin, Robert (date)
　How to find hidden real estate bargains.

　Includes index.
　1. Real estate investment.　I. Title.
HD1382.5.I73　1986　　　　332.63′24　　　　85-24101
ISBN 0-07-032122-1

1 2 3 4 5 6 7 8 9 0　D O C / D O C　8 9 3 2 1 0 9 8 7 6

ISBN 0-07-032122-1

*The editors for this book were Martha Jewett and Martha Cameron,
the designer was Naomi Auerbach, and the production supervisor was
Teresa F. Leaden. It was set in Primer by Crane Typesetting*

Printed and bound by R. R. Donnelley & Sons Company

DISCLAIMER

This book contains the author's opinion on the subject. Neither the author nor
the publisher is engaged in offering legal, tax, accounting, investment, or similar
professional services. Some material may be affected by changes in the law or
in the interpretation of laws since the book was written. Laws also vary from
state to state. Therefore, no guarantee can be given as to the accuracy and
completeness of information. In addition, recommendations made by the author
as well as strategies outlined in the text may not necessarily be suitable depending
on changes or new interpretations of the law or depending upon a reader's personal financial situation. For legal, tax, accounting, investment, or other professional advice, it is suggested that the reader consult a competent practitioner.
The author hereby specifically disclaims any liability for loss incurred as a con-
sequence of any material presented in this book.

Contents

Preface

The first question that probably came to your mind when you saw the title of this book was, "Are there still any real estate bargains out there?"

This book promises a lot and, given the recent ups and downs of the real estate market, it's only natural to wonder about its credibility. "Does this author really know something, or is it another one of those 'dream' books?" You know the kind—they speculate on what you might be able to do, but never really show you how to do it because it can't *really* be done.

When I began writing this book, I was worried about this reaction for two reasons. First, because of the spate of seminar leaders and financial gurus who have been promising the world to those who invest in real estate, maybe people just wouldn't believe there were any bargains left out there. And second, maybe they were right!

I've been personally involved in real estate for nearly 25 years, first as a broker and then as an investor. But in the very recent past, I hadn't been out there looking for those bargain properties. What if they really weren't available anymore? I felt I couldn't justify writing a book such as this until I had tested today's market myself.

I took 5 weeks to do it. I tried each of the many techniques described in this book. And I'm here to tell you that, without question, the hidden bargains are still out there.

With only a few exceptions, virtually every example of a property used in this book comes directly from bargains I found during the short period of time I was investigating. I purchased three bargain properties during this period of time. In each case the property was substantially below market price, the down payment was low (usually 10 percent), and the interest rate on the financing averaged 2 to 3 points below market. Almost all of the other properties mentioned in this book were purchased either by associates or by other investors.

I don't know if you yourself can also find hidden bargains. Perhaps for some reason you can't follow the procedures outlined. Maybe you're not willing to invest the time (remember, I only spent 5 weeks at it!) or the energy. But I do know that if I were to go out and spend another 5 weeks looking right now, I would come home with at least three more bargain properties.

I sincerely believe it will be well worth the small price of this book for you to try doing it, too.

Robert Irwin

How to Find Hidden Real Estate Bargains

1

How to Find a Bargain

Do bargains in real estate really exist?

Depending on who you ask, you can expect answers from two widely differing viewpoints. On the one hand, a promoter might say, "Real estate bargains are everywhere. They're right under our noses. In fact, there aren't enough investors to take them all!"

On the other hand, there's the viewpoint represented by a woman I recently talked with. She said, "I just called 11 real estate companies and asked them if they had any bargains. Without exception, they told me that if they knew of any bargains, they would buy them up themselves! There aren't any bargains out there for me!"

Which viewpoint is correct? The answer lies somewhere between the two.

Do Bargains Really Exist?

Yes, there are indeed real estate bargains available today.

No, they aren't easy to find.

Yes, you can take advantage of many of them, regardless of how much cash you may have.

No, you probably won't stumble onto them simply by calling a list of brokers and asking for bargains.

Yes, you can find them if you know where to look.

We'll discuss how to locate these bargains later in this chapter, but first (and this is a big *but*) before you can find a bargain you have to be able to recognize one when you see it. I can recall showing a large old house on an R-2 lot (zoned for two dwellings on the property) to an investor who I hoped would buy it with me. When we got out of the car, he walked around the house and commented that it was in run-down condition, the seller was asking too much for the neighborhood, it wasn't in the world's best location, and the financing was terrible. In the short space of 5 minutes, he gave me several excellent reasons why he would never live in the "dump."

But, I pointed out, the lot was R-2. "R2, G2, who cares?" he said. "I'm just not interested in investing in junk real estate. Show me a clean house in a good area and we'll talk."

Later that day I showed the same property to a different investor. She didn't even bother to look around it. All she wanted to know was whether it was zoned R-2. I said it was.

We bought the property, "split" the house (divided it, making it into two separate rentable units), and sold it as a duplex within a short time for a substantial profit.

Moral? The first investor didn't know a bargain when he saw one. The second did. There's no way you can find a bargain if you don't know what to look for.

The Three-Bedroom, Two-Bathroom Dream Bargain

Of course that's not to say that real estate bargains are limited to splits. There's everything from repos to tax auctions; from probates to discounted seconds; from "junk" locations to million-dollar "fixers." We'll look into all of these areas and more in this book, but first let's see how good you are at recognizing a bargain when you see it.

Would you recognize a bargain if you saw it? To help find out, try answering the following question. The way you answer reflects how you visualize what constitutes a bargain in the real estate market.

Question: What does a typical real estate bargain look like? No, it's not a trick question. But it is an important one.

I've asked that question to many, many people. Here's the most common answer I've received: "The typical real estate bargain is a three-bedroom, two-bathroom house that probably needs paint and minor repairs and is located in a fairly good neighborhood but is selling for way below market price."

Was your answer something similar? If so, it's perfectly understandable. This is a bargain that we *all* can recognize. A good home, a good neighborhood, a little fixing, and a low, low price. It's a sweet deal that *anybody* would take in a minute.

Of course, that's the problem: If we have a good house that's in a good location and is easy to fix up, why should it sell for way below market price?

This is not to say it couldn't happen. Seller's distress (discussed in Chapter 9) might result in a lower price for an immediate sale. However, chances are that such a house will sell easily enough for market price, or perhaps at just slightly below market for a very quick sale.

Keep an Open Mind

My point is that if the only bargain you recognize is the dream home we've just discussed, you may be waiting in a very long line. If for some strange reason the owner were willing to sell for dramatically below market price (say 15 or 20 percent), there would be hordes of investors (including many real estate agents) who would scoop it up in a second. You may wait 5 years and never get the opportunity to buy such a property. You could wait 10 years.

On the other hand, if you're willing to take a more open-minded approach—if you're willing to look at *any* piece of real estate and try to find how you can make a profit on it—then you could likely find a suitable bargain this very week.

What I'm asking is that for the rest of this book you put aside any preconceived notions about what a real estate bargain has to be. Instead, be prepared to consider properties that are way above what you might think of as your price range and those that are in what you might formerly have thought of as "horrible" areas. Look for properties that have incredible payments as well as those you have to bid for at public auctions. We're going to look for the bargain in all kinds and types of properties. And we're going to see how it's possible to buy many of those properties and make a profit regardless of how much money you have to invest or what payments you think you can afford.

Develop a Style

However, this is not to say that you will always be looking for bargains in a wide variety of types of real estate. Most successful bargain hunters develop a "style." They find a particular type of property which they can easily understand and work, and then they specifically hunt for it.

However, until you know what your own style is, keep an open mind. Be prepared to look at *all* types of real estate. Don't start excluding properties until you've made a thorough examination of what's out there and of the benefits they offer you.

"I Wouldn't Live in That!"

Finally, *don't* try to find bargain property based on where you would or would not live. (There are two important exceptions to this that we'll get to later in the book.) It could be a one-room shack or a 15-room mansion, a pizza parlor or a six-unit building. Whatever it is, it's an investment— and probably not your first choice for a personal residence.

If you're buying stock, you don't judge the company on the basis of whether or not you would live in the home office. If you're buying commodities, you don't judge your purchase on the basis of whether you personally drink orange juice or eat soybeans. Similarly, if you're buying bargain real estate, don't judge it on the basis of whether or not you personally would live in it. Rather, look at it in the cold light of profit or loss. Your motivation should be "Can I make money on this property?" If you can, consider it. If not, dump it.

Locating Bargain Areas

Now let's get on to locations. Where are the bargain locations, those areas that have bargain properties?

As we'll see, any area at all can have bargain properties. However, we are frequently looking not just for bargains but for *affordable* bargains. We want to find something that we have the money to handle. While for some of us that may mean bidding on very expensive properties, for most of us bargain hunting involves looking for less expensive real estate. Nevertheless, chances are that the ideal piece of property for us is located nearby.

Finding Cheap Properties in Expensive Areas

To see what I mean, let's consider a real challenge—finding less expensive real estate in a big city. What do you do if, for example, you're living in New York City or Los Angeles or some similar metropolitan area where the surrounding real estate may be very expensive? We all know that the day of the $100,000 plus house is upon us in many areas of the country. If we want *cheaper* real estate, how do we find it?

The answer is that, almost without exception, there is cheaper (or more expensive) property nearby regardless of where we live. If you look, you can almost surely find a cheaper (or more expensive) area in which to hunt. If you don't believe this, try the following experiment.

Buy Close to Home

Get a map of your local area and a drawing compass. Put one end of the compass on your home's location on the map, and extend the compass so that it can draw a circle with a 50-mile radius (if your map's scale is 1 inch for 10 miles, then open the compass to 5 inches). Now draw a circle with a 50-mile radius around your home. Anything within that circle is probably not much more than an hour away and is a suitable bargain-hunting territory for you. Forget anything outside the circle.

It would be a rare area of the country indeed that did not have a wide variety of property located within a circle with a 50-mile radius. (We are, after all, talking about over 7500 square miles!) Even if your residence is located within an area of expensive property, somewhere in some direction no more than 50 miles out you're likely to find an area with much less expensive property. The opposite also works—you can usually find a much more expensive area than yours within the circle.

Once you've found an area that feels comfortable, stake it out. Get to know it. Farm it. Claim it as yours. If you're going to find bargains there, you'd better get to know that area better than anyone else does.

I always advocate buying real estate that is as close to my home as possible. The reason is that I can be nearby if there are any maintenance or management problems. In any event, the property should be no farther than I can comfortably drive within an hour or so. (The exception here is that you may know of an excellent property manager in a distant location.) I therefore estimate, that what I buy should be no more than about 50 miles from my home.

What about the Competition?

Some bargain hunters are overwhelmed by the thought of competition. "There must be dozens, hundreds, thousands of other bargain hunters out there. They may be more experienced than I am. They may be brokers and attorneys. What chance do I have?"

My standard reply is "Damn the competition—full speed ahead!" In real estate, I've found that the best way to handle the competition is to ignore it. This is particularly effective, since in most cases the competition is mainly in our minds.

Yes, other brokers and investors will indeed be in competition with you, but not all of them at the same time. Once you limit your location and discover the type of property you want (your style), you'll find that you've eliminated 90 percent of your competition. As for that 10 percent that remains, not all of them will be actively looking on the same day you are. Some will already have found bargains and will be out of the market. Some won't have the cash or financial resources available when the bargain appears. And others won't be looking at just the spot you happen to be when you discover your bargain.

Don't Underestimate Inertia

Never underestimate the power of inertia. Few of us really put forth the energy to get us off dead center. While you're out there actually looking, chances are that 99 percent of your remaining competition is sitting home thinking about looking.

All of which is to say that when you find your bargains, you will often discover that you're all alone, that there's nobody else around at the moment competing with you. I've certainly found that to be the case.

Of course, you don't want to hesitate, because bargains are like honey. Just as honey attracts bees and flies, bargains will eventually attract other investors and treasure hunters. You have to be ready to act immediately.

Get a Game Plan

Finally, you need a plan. In many respects this is the single most important asset a bargain hunter can have.

Do you need a game plan to win at real estate bargains? Think of it this way. The San Francisco 49ers or the Chicage Bears or some other top pro football team comes to the stadium for the Superbowl. Just before the game they huddle around the coach, who says to them, "Let's get out there and win!"

The players give a cheer. Then, as they run out onto the field, one of the tight ends asks the quarterback, "What are we going to do? What's our game plan?" The quarterback shrugs his shoulders and says, "I don't know. We'll just pass the ball around a bit and see what happens."

Sure they will . . . and at the end of the game they'll be down by 40 points. In order to win, football teams have a plan, a strategy that they follow. Usually the team with the best plan wins.

Bargain Game Plans

It's the same in business, and particularly in real estate. *It's not enough just to look for and find bargains.* You must have a plan for what to do once you've found the bargain.

A very successful bargain hunter I know *never* buys a piece of real estate, no matter how much of a bargain it seems to be, until he has what he calls a firm "escape plan" in mind. What he's speaking about, of course, is a plan for getting rid of the property and collecting his profits. Here are some typical game plans, or escape plans, for real estate bargains:

1. Immediately resell the property for a profit.
2. Hold it long-term and rent it out for cash flow and/or tax benefits.
3. Refinance it to get your cash out; then hold or dump it.
4. Trade it for other property.

The game plan should be thought out well in advance of a purchase. For example, if your plan for a particular property is to resell it quickly, you should see to it that *when you make your purchase* the financing is easily assumed by the next buyer so that you will be able to get out quickly.

Or, if your game plan is to hold it long-term, you should see to it that the payments are sufficiently low that you won't have a negative cash flow. (As investors know, a negative cash flow means that your expenses exceed your income.)

The investor friend I mentioned advocates having at least *two* escape plans—one long-term and one short-term. Your short-term plan may be to resell quickly. But if for some reason that proves impossible, your long-term plan may involve being able to hold and rent the property until such time as you can sell it.

Throwing Money at Real Estate Won't Work Anymore

The last thing you want to do is to expend all your energy buying a bargain only to find that once you have it, you don't know what to do with it. The days when you could just buy a property, wait 3 months, and then quickly resell it for a substantial profit are long gone. To succeed today, you not only need to know how to get in; you also need to know how to get out.

As I'm sure you're aware, we've only scratched the surface on finding hidden bargains. But that, after all, is the topic of this book. In the next chapters we'll go into ways to find specific bargains, such as repos or fixers. But first let's take a look at the seven different items to look for in a bargain.

2

Seven Things to Look for in a Bargain

What makes one piece of property a bargain and another not? I've found that there are seven critical areas that *must* be considered every time we look for real estate bargains. It's important to understand that we're talking here about *investing,* not about buying for our own residence; when we buy for ourselves, the considerations will surely be different.

Why must we examine these seven areas? The seven are those which I, and other investors I've talked with, have found to be vital. Taking these into consideration can lead us to high profits. On the other hand, failure to consider any one of them could result in an investment disaster.

The seven areas to watch out for are:

1. *Price.* The property sells for substantially below market.
2. *Terms.* The down payment, interest rate, terms, or other conditions of financing are below market.
3. *Rental and resale market.* The property is mistakenly positioned in either of these markets.
4. *Location.* The location is actually better than the seller acknowledges.
5. *Condition.* It's a "distressed" property that you can fix up.
6. *Zoning.* The zoning provides an opportunity to put the property to a higher and better use.
7. *Occupancy.* It's vacant and there's no problem; or it's occupied, you can't get the tenant out, and this is a big problem.

If you're familiar with real estate transactions (or have read books on real estate investment), you've probably seen these seven mentioned in one or more contexts. I seriously doubt, however, that you've seen all of them listed together or placed in this priority.

Note, for example, that I have listed location as number 4. Yet all real estate agents and investors who know their salt have been taught that location is the prime factor in real estate. In fact, the most important rule when buying real estate has always been location, location, location!

Not anymore! Especially not when we're looking for bargain property. Here location is but one of many factors; others, such as price, terms, and market, can be far more important.

To put it differently, when you first bargain hunt you'll probably have to change many preconceived notions you may have about investing in property. I suggest that you carry a small piece of paper with the above list written on it. That way, each time you check out a piece of property, you can go down the list and be sure you haven't left something important out.

Understanding the Big Seven

To be a winner, a property has to be outstanding in at least one of the first six areas. To avoid being a disaster, a property has to have no negatives in any of the seven areas.

If the above judgment seems arbitrary, rest assured that it isn't. I arrived at this list of seven after having gone through many cases, including some instances of bitter experience. The rules to follow are simple:

RULE 1: *The property must be outstanding in at least one of the first six areas.*

RULE 2: *The property should have no overwhelming problem in any of the remaining areas.*

For the remainder of this chapter we are going to examine in detail each of the seven critical areas. We'll look at examples and learn how to recognize benefits as well as problems.

I realize that many readers are more anxious to get into the bargains themselves than to dwell on the theory of bargain hunting. Therefore, if you first want to check into the kinds of hidden real estate bargains that are available, you may skip ahead to the next chapter. I do suggest, however, that at some time before starting your bargain hunting in the real world in earnest, you finish reading this chapter. It contains much vital information and many clues on pitfalls to avoid.

Price

Everyone recognizes a price bargain. It means that you're getting a piece of property at below market value. If comparable houses are going for $90,000 and you can buy one for $80,000, it would seem logical to say that as soon as you've made your purchase, you've acquired a $10,000 profit:

Market value	$90,000
Purchase price	80,000
Profit	$10,000

Of course, it really isn't that simple. If you've had any experience at all in real estate, you quickly realize that there's usually a catch when the price is low. There is some problem that is causing the low price. It might turn out that the property requires expensive work and that $10,000 below market isn't enough of a price cut to make it worth buying. Or it may be that our game plan calls for a quick resale, yet the costs of resale will eat up the whole $10,000. Consequently, what may at first seem to be a profit could in reality be a loss.

The point is that just because the price is low doesn't necessarily make the property a bargain. We need to avoid "price fixation"; that is, we have to avoid thinking that just because it's below market, it's a good deal. Maybe it is, and then again maybe it isn't. Here are three problems to watch out for when determining whether a property priced for below market value is truly a bargain:

1. Hidden problems with the property
2. Underestimated costs of liquidation
3. Invalid estimate of true market value

If none of these problems exists, then you may have a terrific bargain on your hands. You may have gotten what everyone is looking for! On the other hand, if even one of the problems exists, watch out!

Let's take these one at a time.

Hidden Problems

P. T. Barnum is reported to have said, "There's a sucker born every minute." The question with regard to a house with a low price is, who's the sucker? Is it the seller for selling low? Or is it us for buying without knowing why the seller's offering a low price?

The rule is: *Never buy for less than market price until you know exactly why the seller is willing to cut the price.*

Here, along with their value to us, are the most common reasons a seller would be willing to take a lower price:

Why Seller Is Willing to Take a Low Price	*Value to Us*
1. The property is condemned.	0
2. The property will cost at least as much to fix up as the amount by which the seller is reducing the price.	0
3. The seller is desperate to sell.	10
4. The resale market is terrible right now.	5
5. The seller is stupid and doesn't know the property's true value (like finding a living dinosaur).	1
6. The property is in bad shape (but we know how to fix it up for next to nothing).	10
7. We don't know why.	-10

In other words, there are usually only two and a half good reasons for a reduced price that are of benefit to us: The seller is desperate for a quick sale *or* the property is a fixer-upper that we know how to fix up better than the seller does *or* the market is so terrible that the seller has to cut the price and we can buy and hold for a long time (I don't recommend this). I did give 1 point for finding sellers who don't know the true value of their property; however, today almost all sellers have an inflated idea of their property's value, not the other way around.

If we find a property with any of the good reasons present, then we should consider buying. On the other hand, if the seller has one of the other reasons for selling lower—or if we don't know the reason—then we should walk away from the deal.

Underestimated Costs of Liquidation

Assuming that we are indeed fortunate enough to buy a property for substantially below market price, have we then immediately made a profit?

Not necessarily. Remember, we don't actually make our money until we sell the property and receive our check. If our plan for the property consists of buying and then quickly reselling, the liquidation costs could eat up our potential profit. There's an old rule in real estate that any agent can vouch for: Don't count the money until it's in your pocket.

Consider our example: Given that the market value is $90,000 and we buy for $80,000, have we really made a $10,000 profit? Before we can pocket the $10,000 we will probably need to resell the house. (We'll talk about refinancing and "crankables" in Chapter 13.) While we can indeed do this on our own either as a "for sale by owner" (FSBO) or as a trade, in many cases we'll need the services of an agent in order to get a quick, clean sale, particularly in a tight market (we'll see other important reasons to use an agent as we go along). This means that we'll need to pay the agent a commission. There may also be closing costs, mortgage payments, and fix-up costs:

Commission	$5400
Closing costs	2000
Mortgage payments	1000
Fix-up costs	500
Liquidation costs	$8900

What should be obvious is that, when we subtract the $8900 in potential costs involved in realizing that profit, we find we've only made about $1100 instead of a $10,000 profit. This $1100 isn't bad, but it isn't quite the treasure we thought we'd get.

But it could have been *if* we'd gotten into the property at a lower price, say, $70,000 instead of $80,000. Buying for $20,000 less than market value makes it a real bargain. At that much less, after our roughly $9000 in expenses we could still get an $11,000 profit.

Remember, just because a property is priced below market doesn't mean it's a good deal. It's the amount below market *after* liquidation costs that counts.

Invalid Estimate of Market Value

Finally, when we come across a surprisingly low price, we have to be sure that there really is value there. We have to be wary that maybe it might only be our interpretation of the price that's low. In other words, do we really know what the true market value of the property is?

"Market value" is a wonderful term. It implies precision and knowledge. But in truth it's nothing more than an educated guess.

What is the true market value of any property? It's what a buyer is willing to pay for it. Without a buyer, the property has *no* market value.

When you're looking for a price bargain, be sure that you estimate a property's market value on the basis of the best evidence. Go to a nearby real estate agent and ask to see "comparables," data on recent sales of similar properties. Most real estate agencies are computerized and can get this information for you in a matter of minutes.

Accurately estimating the true market value does take time and does require good judgment, but it's an essential part of bargain hunting.

To sum up, these are the three areas to watch out for when you are searching for a price bargain: A property can only be a bargain in terms of price when it has no hidden problems, when you've taken its liquidation costs into account, and when you know its true market value.

Terms

We've already mentioned that many buyers and even more sellers are hung up on price. Their feeling is that the *only* thing that counts in real estate is the sales price. Nothing could be further from the truth (but try telling that to an adamant seller). Consequently, it is sometimes easier to give the seller the full price and instead insist on wonderful terms. I find it positively amazing how some sellers will agree to what are horrendous terms for them just as long as they get their price. This is called a "terms bargain," or "financing bargain."

How can a property be a bargain if we get good terms yet pay the full price? It's easy.

A Terms Bargain

An investor I know recently found a financing bargain. Josh located a four-unit apartment building for which the seller was asking $200,000. Josh determined that each unit was rented out for $500 per month. That brought in a gross income for the whole year of $24,000.

Josh knew that the value of apartment buildings is directly dependent on the income. He used a rule-of-thumb method of calculating: He divided the gross income ($24,000) into the asking price ($200,000) and came up with a multiple of 8.3. The building was selling for 8.3 times its gross.

Josh had studied the comps (comparable properties) and had discovered that a multiple of 8.3 was a bit high. Most other similar buildings sold for only 8 times their gross annual income, so he offered $160,000 for the building. The seller turned down the offer and refused to make a counter offer. She wouldn't take a penny less than $200,000. She wanted her slightly inflated price.

When the Owner Won't Cut the Price

Did Josh give up and wash his hands of the deal because he couldn't get a good price? Did he immediately assume that there was no bargain here? Not at all.

What he did was to look at the property to see if it could be a terms bargain. When he examined the financing he found out that the owner had only a single first mortgage of $75,000 on the building. There was no other financing.

Giving Price and Demanding Terms

Josh then offered *full price* with a token down payment of $10,000. (In Chapters 13 and 14 we'll see the problems with offering no down payment in today's market and how to raise the cash we need to make deals like this.) His offer further specified that the seller would agree to carry back the balance in the form of a second mortgage at 7 (yes, 7) percent interest!

Down payment	$10,000
Second mortgage	$110,000
First mortgage	$75,000

Josh's total mortgage payments would be about $1800 per month.

The seller objected that 7 percent interest was way below market. But Josh pointed out that she was getting her full price. She finally agreed to sell.

Josh jumped for joy. He had gotten his price bargain.

Where's the Bargain?

At first glance it might appear that there was no bargain here. After all, Josh had paid full price, which was slightly above market. Yet there was indeed a bargain. Here's how to figure it:

Monthly income from property	$2000
Mortgage payments	1800
Positive cash flow	$ 200

The property will pay for itself. The $200 positive cash flow after mortgages will probably pay most of the tax and insurance costs. By the time Josh takes depreciation and other deductions on his taxes, he may even end up with some cash in his pocket from this rental property.

But the real bargain has to do with rent increases. Rents are increasing across the country. If rents go up 7 percent a year for this building (they're actually going up close to this rate in many parts of the country as of this writing), the property's gross annual income after 5 years would increase to about $33,000. Assuming roughly the same gross multiplier (8 times income), Josh's property would then be worth $264,000.

Old gross income	$24,000
New gross income	33,000
Increase	$ 9,000

Josh bought for $200,000. After 5 years he could probably sell for $264,000. Before liquidation costs he would therefore stand to gross $64,000 on his $10,000 investment.

But there's more. Remember, the rents went up *but* the mortgage payments remained constant. At the fifth year the expenses remained $24,000. But by then the income had grown to $33,000. In the fifth year Josh was pocketing $9000! And that was before his tax write-off!

Big Challenge, Big Profits

Josh only invested $10,000. He was making almost that amount in cash flow on the property by year 5 even before taking into account the profit on a sale. The big cash flow plus the potential sales profit make the property a terrific bargain, a terrific *financing* bargain!

It was all made possible by the terms. In order to get her price, the seller was willing to accept a below-market interest rate and a low down payment. (For the seller's problems with "imputed" interest, see the section "Using Soft Paper to Get Bargains" in Chapter 13.)

A seller who's adamant about price often can't sell and becomes desperate. In such circumstances a terms bargain may be possible. All of which is to say that when we look for bargain real estate, we must get beyond worrying only about price bargains. The financing often makes bargains which are just as good.

Rental and Resale Market

Throughout the world of finance, knowledge means power and money—and the same holds true in bargain real estate. If you know more about the rental or resale market than does the seller, you may be able to use this information to get a bargain. These I call "market bargains." Here are two examples.

A Rental Market Bargain

You've found a six-unit building that is for sale at 8 times the gross annual rent. Each unit is rented out for $300 per month, making the sales price $173,000.

However, you notice that the owner hasn't been watching the rental market. He says that tenants in the area are very transient and that he thus keeps his rents competitive so that his building will always be fully occupied. He worries that if he raises the rents he will get greater vacancies.

However, because you've been analyzing the local rental market carefully, you know that clean units with air conditioning (which these apartments do *not* yet have) are today renting for $450 a month. Given the present scarcity and desirability of such units, you figure that you can keep the building full all the time, keeping your vacancy factor down to virtually zero.

Calculating Current Value

So you buy for $173,000, fix up the units, and add air conditioning. The tenants come and go—and over a year, as the old ones depart, you rent to the new ones at $450. Assuming you're not in a rent control area, when all the units have been rented at the higher price, your total annual income has gone up. Remember, price is a factor of rental rates.

Monthly rent, six units @ $450	$ 2,700
Annual rent ($2,700 × 12)	32,400
Multiplier	× 8
Current value	259,200
Less purchase price	173,000
Gross profit	$ 86,200

Of course, there was the cost of the air conditioning and the fixing up. But if that came to even $1500 a unit, or $9000 total, you've still made a hefty profit of over $77,000 before liquidation costs. Your profit was made possible because you knew more about the rental market than did the seller.

Yes, frequently owners *don't* know the rental market they are in. Once again, it's inertia. They've been renting low for so long that they sometimes assume that it's the only price they can get.

When You Don't Really Know the Market

Of course, the opposite could be true. The seller could be a bit underhanded. To make the income look higher, he might have rented out the units for $450 to relatives and friends. If we were unsophisticated, we might think that since other apartments (those which were fixed up and had air conditioning) were renting for that amount, the rent was fair— and we might thus pay a price based on the $450 rent.

As soon as we bought, however, the friends and relatives could move out and we could find ourselves unable to rerent for more than $300 unless we improved the units. This is a classic case of the seller pulling the wool over the buyer's eyes, and it happens countless times. Be wary of it. Be sure that you're the one who knows the rental market better than the seller does, and not the other way round.

A Resale Market Bargain

You've found a two-bedroom house that's selling for $80,000, which the owner and you agree is the market value. You alone, however, know that the area is desperate for three-bedroom houses and that the same house with three bedrooms would bring $105,000. You have also seen similar houses in which the garage has been converted to a third bedroom and a carport has been added to replace the garage. You know that the total cost for such a conversion will be no more than $5000.

You arrange to buy at a price of $80,000. You then convert for $5000 and thus have a property worth $105,000. As a result, your potential sales profit before liquidation costs is $20,000.

This is a bargain that comes about because you know the resale market.

Location

As I noted earlier, this used to be considered the single most critical factor when buying real estate. Every investor and agent quickly learned that the three rules of property were *location, location, location!*

This is certainly still true if we're buying for our own residence. But with bargain hunting, the three items just covered (price, terms, and market) can be more important. To see the truth of this, consider the following example.

A Bargain in a Poor Location

We find a house in good condition that is selling for $50,000 under market value, but it's in the worst neighborhood in town. Should we *not* buy it because of its poor location? Note that the price is $50,000 *under* market value. Presumably this market value *already* takes the neighborhood into account. In other words, the house is selling for $50,000 less than comparable houses are selling for, even in this undesirable area.

Let's put it another way. A house in a highly desirable area might sell for $150,000, but in a very undesirable area it might sell for half. But if we can buy that house in the undesirable area for $25,000, should we pass it up because of its location? True, we might only be able to resell it for $75,000. But should we turn our noses up at a $50,000 profit because the location isn't a top one? (I only use the $50,000 profit figure for illustration; but price bargains often occur in less desirable neighborhoods, whereas they are seldom found in top areas.)

I hope you see the point. When we bargain hunt, location is a factor, but not the only or the most important factor. Were we to be buying a house for ourselves to live in, then I would put location right up there at the top. But if we're bargain hunting, then there are other considerations such as a price, terms, and market that, quite frankly, can be more important.

Negative Locations

There is a negative side to location, however, that we must also consider. Sometimes the location of a specific property is so negative that we will want to eliminate it from consideration. For example, the houses in a certain neighborhood may be selling for $60,000 and we find one there—the same model as the others—selling for $40,000. So it's a bargain, right?

Maybe not *if* the house happens to be one of the few in the tract that is right across the street from an undesirable element, say a factory. I saw this exact example not long ago. It was a tract of about 300 houses all in the price range mentioned. One end of the tract, however, bordered for only one block on an industrial area. Directly across the street from about six houses was a manufacturing plant. In addition to the factory-like setting (cyclone fence, weed-grown yard with greasy and broken machinery lying about, and workers parking cars on the street), the factory also exhausted noxious fumes, some of which drifted directly into the houses across the street.

Anywhere else in the tract, that $40,000 house might be worth $60,000 but when it was right in front of that factory, it really wasn't worth more than it was priced. In this case the location proved to be a significant negative factor.

Condition

When I talk about condition, I'm really talking about what is commonly called a "fixer-upper." In Chapter 9, "Distressed Properties," we'll go into the pluses and minuses of the field, how to find such homes, and how to price them.

For now, let's just say that it's often possible to find a property whose price is less because of its distressed condition. If we're willing (either with our sweat or by hiring out the work) to buy at the low price and fix the property up, we can frequently make a profit.

Let's not consider those properties priced just under their market value because of a slightly distressed condition. If all that a house needs is paint and some carpeting, the seller may simply have subtracted the price of those items from the sales price. For example, the market value should be $125,000, but the house needs $3000 in painting and carpeting, so the seller has priced the house at $120,000. If we buy, we'll still have to spend the $3000, so in this case we might earn $2000 for our efforts. To my way of thinking, the effort just isn't worth the money, particularly when we consider the liquidation costs.

The really big profits come when the property is truly distressed. The house is slipping down a hillside and is condemned. Were it on sound footing, it would be worth $350,000, but because of its present condition it's going for $75,000. Can we buy it, somehow inexpensively fix it up, and sell it for a profit?

Or say that the property's market value should be $100,000 but that the house's plumbing is corroded, its roof needs replacing, and it has to be replastered inside. It's selling for $50,000. Can we go in and do the work for next to nothing and reap a big profit? We'll examine these and other factors when we look into distressed properties in Chapter 9.

Here, however, the critical factor comes down to one thing. Is the physical problem with the house solvable or not? The rule is that, if we can't solve the problem, we shouldn't buy. But if we can solve the problem, then we should seriously consider the property.

Zoning

Surprisingly, this is an area that most investors tend to ignore. Yet it's one that can frequently yield substantial profits from bargains.

In the first example in this book, I explained how a house turned out to be a bargain because it was on an R-2, or duplex zoned, lot. It was bought, split, and sold for a much higher price.

The same holds true for industrial and commercial property. In real estate it's called considering the highest and best use for property.

"Highest and best use" means that the owner is getting the most out of the land. If we have a lot zoned for three units and there is only a single house on it, then it's not getting its highest and best use. If we have a lot zoned commercial and there's a three-unit residential building on it, it's not getting its highest and best use (which would probably be some sort of store). If it's zoned for office buildings and it only has a storage garage on it, it's not getting its highest and best use.

Underutilized Properties Mean Bargains

Bargains can occur when we discover a property that is underutilized. Since the price is usually based on *current* utilization (with perhaps something thrown in for potential), we may be able to buy low, convert to a higher use, and resell high. In our example, we bought a single-family residence and converted it to a duplex. By changing the property to a higher use, we increased the value and hence made our profit.

In most areas of the country, property that has been built in the last 20 or 30 years has been constructed in accordance with its highest or best use. Developers have been keenly aware of costs and have built to get the most out of the land. If it's zoned for three units and it's a recent structure, chances are that you'll find three units on it.

Look for Older Properties

But older property isn't always that way, particularly property built prior to or just after World War II. For some reason, builders of that era frequently underutilized the lots, building single-family homes on multiple-zoned or commercial or even industrial property. In addition, sometimes the zoning in an area has changed over the years, producing the same result.

What that means to us is a potential bonanza in zoning, particularly with older property. The key is spending the time to find underutilized property.

Watch Out for Midnight Conversions

Of course, many times others will have beat us to it. Current or former owners may have made "midnight conversions" (done without benefit of local building department approval). Garages, for instance, may have been converted to a second unit on a duplex lot. Beware of these.

This frequently happens in older areas or where the zoning has changed. But not always. Sometimes we can find property which has the right zoning and which hasn't been converted. We can buy, convert, and take the profit.

Learn to Read the Zoning Maps

To do this, of course, we need to know what the zoning is. The planning department of our city, county, township, or other government body has maps which pinpoint the zoning for every property in our area. These are often huge, cumbersome maps. But they are available to the public, and we can go down and make copies.

In addition, publishing companies that print city maps often print ones which include zoning references. These can usually be purchased at local stationery stores. Sometimes real estate boards will offer them to the public (either directly or through member brokers) as a service.

I always try to carry a zoning map when I go out scouting for bargains. Knowing the zoning could make a difference in finding a real treasure.

Watch Out for Zoning Errors

There is, unfortunately, a negative side to zoning. Sometime the maps are wrong and sometimes property owners are wrong in their knowledge of their land's zoning. If we buy a property thinking that it's R-2, only to find that it's really R-1, we could be in for a big loss.

I recently avoided such a problem by carefully checking with the city. I was looking at a property that was 50 feet wide by 250 feet long. It had a house on the front and two small potential rental units behind. The property was zoned R-3, meaning in this case that it could be used for up to three units, yet it was only being used for one. As a single-unit lot, its asking price was $112,000. However, as a multiple lot with three units rented out (converting the guest houses to rentals) it could be worth $50,000 to $75,000 more. My map clearly showed that it was R-3. Had I found a bargain?

Experience has taught me prudence. I went to the zoning department and rechecked on their enlarged maps. Yes, the first 20 feet of the lot was indeed zoned R-3. However, everything back of the first 20 feet was zoned R-1. The lot had two zones on it and was totally unsuitable for more than one dwelling! Had I purchased hoping to take advantage of a higher use, I would have found my hopes dashed.

All of which is to say that zoning is a double-edged sword. If you're going to play the zoning game, be sure you know exactly what you're getting into. Yes, you can get real bargains here. But the unwary can also get hurt.

In addition, zoning should be a consideration *anytime you look at bargain property. Be sure there isn't a big negative in the zoning that overwhelms the property's other positives.*

Occupancy

This is like a veto. Occupancy doesn't usually add to the allure of a bargain property, but if it's going to be a problem, it can be a good reason to avoid the real estate.

Regardless of what our game plan for a property may be, one thing we will almost always want to do is to rent the property out. Rental income to offset mortage and other expenses is a must in investment real estate. The question is, can we rent it out? Or is there someone occupying the property who won't get out and who won't pay rent?

At first glance this may appear to be nothing more than a minor problem. There are eviction laws ("unlawful detainer") in all states; they come first on court dockets, they are relatively inexpensive to promote, and they work fairly fast. So what's the problem? If a tenant won't pay and won't get out, we evict.

It's not that simple. There are three possible problems with occupancy.

1. We can't evict tenants because they are protected by rent control laws. (The tenants could claim that we're evicting just so we can raise the rent—and we could be subject to a lengthy court case, and if we lose, to severe penalties.)

2. The occupants say they have an ownership claim on the property and defend it in court. The court action is lengthy.

3. The occupants are ill or pregnant and claim that they can't be moved without sustaining physical injury.

If you haven't run into these problems on your own, rest assured that others have. The first and third listed here are fairly obvious, but let's consider the second.

When the Occupant Cries "Fraud!"

We buy a house at a foreclosure sale. It's a real bargain—we get it for half of its market value. However, the former owner is still occupying the property. She says there was fraud in the foreclosure and refuses to move out.

We know that the claim of fraud is ridiculous, so we start an unlawful detainer action to get her evicted. Normally this takes only a week or two. And normally the defendant in an unlawful detainer eviction doesn't show up, but in this case our former owner does show up. She claims that she was tricked into signing the former mortgage—that there was fraud—that the property should rightfully still be hers.

Fraud? Trickery? No judge is going to dismiss such charges out of hand. The case is held over. Now the legal battle begins. She hires an attorney, who takes depositions, makes motions, demands a jury trial, and moves the case from one court to another.

Note that we're not saying the former owner has a legitimate case. She only has the desire not to leave the property. She stays there, not paying us rent.

Weeks drag on into months as our attorney fees go up. In the case I'm thinking of, the investor ultimately spent $30,000 in legal and court costs and it took 9 months to get the former owner out of the property. During that time, his money was tied up in the house and he didn't get a penny of rent. He says the only reason he finally persevered was because she ran out of money to keep paying her own attorney.

Occupancy Can Veto an Otherwise Good Bargain

It can happen. Occupancy can become a critical issue in the purchase of bargain real estate.

Therefore, whenever I consider purchasing a property, I always check to see if it's occupied, are the tenants paying rent, and will they move if I want them to?

The easiest way to handle this is to demand as a condition of purchase that the property be vacant at the close of escrow (time of sale). There shall be no evidence (furnishings, clothing, or anything else) of any occupant in the property. Even if this means displacing a paying tenant, sometimes it's the safest thing to do.

On the other hand, sometimes you can't get occupancy for one reason or another. (In our above example of a foreclosure, we as the buyer have no control over occupancy until we get title to the property.) In such cases, we have to go on what we can see and use our best judgment.

That's why I list occupancy as a veto factor. If there's a problem here, it could be a reason to forget a would-be bargain that might otherwise have all kinds of advantages.

Putting It All Together

These, then, are the seven areas to watch out for when trying to determine if we've got a bargain. Remember, there's more than just price, and location isn't everything in this kind of property. Each item *must* be considered. Once again, here are the seven items. As I suggested, you

might want to jot these down on a piece of paper to carry with you when
you go bargain hunting:

1. Price
2. Terms
3. Resale and rental market
4. Location
5. Condition
6. Zoning
7. Occupancy

3

Foreclosure
Opportunities

Foreclosure: What is it? How does it happen? Does it provide an opportunity for bargain hunters?

Foreclosure has become a popular concept among real estate bargain hunters. The foreclosure market has always been present. However, in recent years it's gotten a reputation as being the place where the "in" people find the bargains. In a very real sense this is true. In this chapter we're going to focus in on foreclosures, see how to find them, and look at the specific benefits they may offer us.

How Foreclosures Can Be Hidden Treasures

Let's say you've found a neighborhood where the average house sells for about $120,000. If you are bargain hunting, you may hope to find a distressed house or a distressed seller and, if you're lucky, be able to buy for as much as $20,000 below market.

But as you're looking, you notice a house that seems abandoned. The doors are locked, the side windows are boarded up, and the lawn has turned to weeds. Doing some inquiring, you find out that the former owner couldn't make the mortgage payments; consequently, the house is being sold in foreclosure.

Through some careful investigative work (we'll see how shortly), you find out that the house has a $70,000 mortgage on it. You also find out that next week the property will be sold to the highest bidder "on the county courthouse steps."

Of course the lender will bid the full amount of the mortgage, $70,000, since that's how much he has in the house. But could you bid $70,100 and get the property?

If you could, think of what a steal it would be. You'd be getting a house for virtually $50,000 under market price! That's far better than any deal you are likely to be able to negotiate with a seller. Now that's a bargain!

Does It Happen?

Is our example true to life? Do foreclosures occur which have such enormous bargain potential?

The answer is yes. They occur all the time in almost all areas of the country. Even during boom times there are some foreclosures, but in recent years the foreclosure rate has risen enormously. At times it has hovered near the rate of 1 percent of all properties available, which would put it at the highest point since the great depression.

There are several reasons for the high foreclosure rate. Foremost among these are the many buyers who purchased for little or no down payment back in 1980 and 1981. They bought hoping to take advantage of the rapid price appreciation in real estate. However, between 1981 and 1985 there was virtually no price appreciation in most residential real estate in this country. In fact, prices declined in many areas.

The result has been that many buyers who overleveraged their properties with short-term, high-interest-rate mortgages have found themselves in a bind in recent years. These mortgages were coming due; however, their properties hadn't gone up in value. They suddenly found that in order to keep the properties they would have to either refinance (costly) or come up with plenty of cash (more costly). Since the properties hadn't appreciated, neither alternative seemed appealing; consequently, many such owners just "walked." They left their properties and allowed them to go to foreclosure.

Add to the above group the many other individuals who abandoned their property because of divorce, loss of job, bankruptcy, death, or other causes, and you have a large supply of foreclosures out there.

Are They All Bargains?

Most definitely not. Only a small portion of foreclosures are really bargains—yet this is probably the most misunderstand fact in the whole field. There are too many investors who simply think that because a property can be labeled a "foreclosure," it's a bargain.

In our example of the house with a $70,000 mortgage, the property was truly a bargain, since it could be obtained for so much below its market price. But, as noted, many of the foreclosures available today occurred because of overleveraging—buying with little or no down payment.

This means that the mortgage(s) on the property are often worth close to the full market value. Sometimes the mortgage(s) are worth more than the property is!

Here's an example. Let's say we investigated the above property, and we found that it had a second and a third mortgage in addition to its $70,000 first mortgage.

First	$ 70,000
Second	30,000
Third	25,000
	$125,000

The lender of the third was foreclosing. If we were to buy the property at foreclosure now, we'd end up paying $125,000, or about $5000 more than market value.

That's no bargain, yet it's still a foreclosure sale.

The Foreclosure Process

In order to determine whether or not a foreclosure is really a bargain, it's necessary to understand the foreclosure process. It's been my experience that most people who dabble in foreclosures (including many agents) really don't know enough about what's going on. Yet if there's one area where expert knowledge is necessary, this is it.

The easiest way to understand the foreclosure process is to think of it in stages.

Stage 1: Borrower Can't (or Won't) Make Payments

If the borrower doesn't make the payments, then the lender's recourse is to take back the property. Following a legal process, which varies according to which state you are in, the lender starts foreclosure proceedings.

Stage 2: Property Is Publicly Sold

At the end of the foreclosure proceedings, the property is sold to the highest bidder at a public auction. At this sale, *anyone* can bid; however, the sale is normally for cash, and since the lender can always bid the amount of money that he or she has already loaned on the house, the lender is usually the first bidder.

Stage 3: Lender Owns the Property

If the lender is the only bidder, then after the sale it is the lender who owns the property. (Former owner may have redemption rights.)

Opportunities to Buy

We can find different opportunities to obtain foreclosures at each stage of the process.

At stage 1 opportunities exist to get the property from the owner at a reduced price. In Chapter 4 we'll go into how to buy the loan (and ultimately the property) by dealing directly with the lender.

At stage 2 there are opportunities available by bidding directly at the foreclosure sale.

At stage 3 we can find bargains by buying the property from a lender who's taken it back after a sale (called REO real estate), which we'll discuss in Chapter 6.

Dealing With an Owner Who's in Foreclosure

We'll be covering stages 2 and 3 in Chapter 5 and 6. For now, let's start with stage 1, dealing with the owner-borrower of the property before public sale. This is the area of foreclosure that most newcomers are interested in; therefore, it's only appropriate that we deal with it first. But be forewarned. This is *not* an area that I recommend!

When dealing with an owner who is in foreclosure, we are naturally going to be curious about many things. How did the owner get into this predicament? What are the owner's options? What opportunities exist for bargains? Let's take an example.

Our owner is Terri. She bought her house a year ago. The purchase price was $100,000. Here's how she paid for it:

| Down payment | $15,000 |
| First mortgage (from S&L) | $85,000 |

Terri had a job from which she made enough money to keep up the payments on her mortgage. However, after about a year she lost her job. Without income, she couldn't make the payments and the mortgage lender started foreclosure.

The foreclosure procedure differs from state to state. In Texas it can be as short as 1 month between the time a notice of default is filed (a formal notice telling the borrower that he or she is in arrears) and the time the house is sold at auction (see Figure 3-1). In California, it takes a little less than 4 months. In some New England states it can take upwards of a year.

In Terri's case, it was nearly 2 months before a notice of default was filed. (Her lenders kept hoping that she would get a job and make up the back payments.)

Since Terri lived in California, she had 3 months and 21 days from the time the default was filed until her property was sold from under her. During that period of time, she continued to occupy the house but did not make any payments. Each day that went by that she couldn't catch up with the payments and penalties drew her closer to losing her property.

It is here that our first bargain opportunity occurs. We can contact Terri directly. Since she is going to lose her house if she doesn't act, we can offer her several options:

1. We can offer to make up the back payments and penalties if she is willing to give us a deed to the property. (Our cost here will probably be only a few thousand dollars.)
2. We can offer to do the above plus give her a set amount of money for her equity (anywhere from a few hundred to a few thousand dollars).
3. We can offer to do the above plus allow her to rent back the property from us (so she won't have to move).

With all of these alternatives there are perils, which we'll discuss shortly; however, should Terri accept any alternatives, we would acquire the property. Our advantage in this case would be that we would get it for substantially less than its market value. (Remember, market value is illusory; see Chapter 2.) In addition, we'd be getting it without sticking in a lot of our own cash.

Here's how we do it in two simple steps.

Step 1: Finding a Property in Foreclosure

The first step, obviously, is finding Terri or someone like her. This isn't really all that difficult.

IMPORTANT NOTICE

IF YOUR PROPERTY IS IN FORECLOSURE BECAUSE YOU ARE BEHIND IN YOUR PAYMENTS, IT MAY BE SOLD WITHOUT ANY COURT ACTION, and you may .have legal right to bring your account in good standing by paying all of your past due payments plus permitted costs and expenses within three months from the date this notice of default was recorded. This amount is   Plus Estimated Fees and Expenses as of   , and will increase until your account becomes current. You may not have to pay the entire unpaid portion of your account, even though full payment was demanded, but you must pay the amount stated above.

However, you and your beneficiary or mortgagee may mutually agree in writing prior to the time the notice of sale is posted (which may not be earlier than the end of the three-month period stated above) to, among other things, (1) provide additional time in which to cure the default by transfer of the property or otherwise; (2) establish a schedule of payments in order to cure your default; or both (1) and (2).

After three months from the date of recordation of this document (which date of recordation appears hereon), unless the obligation being foreclosed upon or a Separate written agreement between you and your creditor permits a longer period, you have only the legal right to stop the Sale of your property by paying the entire amount demanded by your creditor.

To find out the amount you must pay, or to arrange for payment to stop the fore-closure, or if your property is in foreclosure for any other reason, contact:

YOU MAY LOSE LEGAL RIGHTS IF YOU DO NOT TAKE PROMPT ACTION.

If you have any questions, you should contact a lawyer or the government agency which may have insured the loan.

RECORDING REQUESTED BY

AND WHEN RECORDED MAIL TO

NAME

STREET ADDRESS

CITY & STATE

Att

REFERENCE NUMBER

Figure 3–1 Notice of default.

Understanding her own position, Terri will probably have made some effort to liquidate her house. This usually takes the form of putting the house up for sale by owner (FSBO). Initially, to save her good credit and try to recoup some of her investment, she's going to try to sell the property herself.

If we stop at every FSBO we see, pretty soon we're going to run into Terri or someone like her. In a good market where there are lots of buyers,

Terri may very well be able to sell and there won't be much opportunity for bargain hunting. However, if the market is tight (high interest rates restricting buyers), Terri may not be able to sell. If that's the case, then we can find and present our options to her.

The likelihood of Terri accepting our options depends on how close she is to the foreclosure sale. If it's 3 months away, she'll probably not be very interested. If it's tomorrow, she'll pay very close attention to what we say.

Note: Terri may also have listed her property with an agent, in which case our opportunity is considerably diminished. The agent will demand a commission. If it's 6 percent, that's $6000 we would have to pay over and above the back interest and penalties and anything we happened to give Terri. Suddenly it's not so appealing a bargain anymore.

Working with title insurance and trust companies   Another way to find out about cases like Terri's is to contact title insurance companies or trust companies. To understand how this works, we have to understand the foreclosure process in a bit more detail.

In California (and in most but not all states) a legal device called a "trust deed" is used in place of a traditional mortgage. In a traditional mortgage there are only two parties, the borrower and the lender. With a trust deed, however, there are three parties—the borrower (technically, the trustor), the lender (technically, the beneficiary), and the trustee. The trustee holds the power to foreclose and to sell the property. When the borrower doesn't make the payments, the lender tells the trustee, who starts the foreclosure proceedings. To find out about properties in foreclosure, therefore, we need only contact the trustee.

Trustees are usually not individuals, but trust corporations, such as title insurance or trust companies. They usually handle thousands or hundreds of thousands of properties.

Getting a list   Title insurance and trust companies will frequently make available to their "friends," or clients, lists of those properties for which they are trustees and which are in foreclosure. All you have to do is get hold of such a list and go down it. Each person listed is a prospective Terri.

The key here, of course, is to become a client of the trust or title insurance company. How do you become a client? As you invest, you'll be buying and selling a lot of property. Throw your business to a particular title insurance or trust company and you'll quickly achieve client status.

If you haven't yet achieved client status, however, there is another way of getting a list of borrowers who are in foreclosure.

Checking the notices of default   The first step in the foreclosure process is the filing of a notice of default. This is a public notice filed with the county records office. Checking the list at the county recorder's office can be very time-consuming. A shorter route is to check to see if your area has a business or legal paper. Frequently, such a paper will pick up and publish on a weekly basis the notices of default that have been filed.

Finally, if you can't locate such a paper, there are usually services which you can buy (they can be expensive, sometimes $100 per month) which will list all the notices of default that have been filed in your area. Just check with the county recorder's office. They get so many requests that some will keep subscription forms on hand!

Working with a legal description   The disadvantage of getting the property location from the records, from a paper, or from a service is that it's hard to tell where the property is. Usually only a legal description is given (see Figure 3-2). If you've ever seen a legal description, you know that one of the things it doesn't include is the address.

[de]Lot 59 of Tract No. 1043 as per map recorded in
Book 25 Page 46 of Maps, in the office of the County
Recorder, County of Brisbane.[xde]

Figure 3–2 Legal description of a property.

To translate the legal description, you'll probably want either to go back to the recorder's office and look it up (the description will lead to a map on which the streets and addresses can be interpreted) or to take it to your title insurance company, which can quickly give you the same information (which is why I started with the title insurance company at the beginning).

Step 2: Negotiating With the Owner

Once you've located a property in foreclosure and have found someone such as Terri, it becomes a matter of getting the best deal you can. We've already covered the three basic offers you can make Terri. Getting her to accept one usually comes down to demonstrating how it will benefit her.

If you are new to negotiating, I suggest that you check into one of the many books on the subject available in bookstores and libraries. When you do negotiate, however, what's important to remember is the relative positions that you and the owner occupy.

The owner   Terri is probably disgusted, angry, and perhaps a little frightened. Things are going down the drain for her. She is trying to salvage what she can out of a bad situation.

The bargain hunter You want to get in as cheaply as you can. You don't want to offend Terri, however. What you want to do is to stress to her the *benefits* you have to offer. These include:

1. You'll take over the property so she won't have a foreclosure against her name. (Salvaging our good name and credit is important in today's world.)
2. You'll let her live in the house until you take it over.
3. You may give her some cash so she won't have lost everything.

Negotiating comes down to a meeting of the minds. If you can show Terri that the benefits you can offer outweigh waiting any longer, you'll probably get a deal. You'll end up with the house and she'll get her good name, a place to live for awhile longer, and perhaps some cash. (Don't feel you're taking advantage of her. If you weren't there, she'd probably lose the property and her good name, get kicked out, and end up with no cash at all.)

Perils of Dealing With an Owner in Foreclosure

Earlier I noted that there were certain perils in dealing with someone like Terri. Let's look at some of these now.

Statutes Protecting Sellers in Foreclosure

When we offer to make up back payments and penalties in order to get a deed to the property, we may be putting ourselves in jeopardy with state law. Some states (including California) have enacted laws protecting those in foreclosure from being preyed upon by unscrupulous fortune hunters—the kind who might trick Terri into quickly signing over a document transferring title without fully understanding what she was doing and against her own best interests.

Some states give the seller a 5-day period of recision when signing over property that is in default. In some cases the redemption period can be a year or longer! Be sure you know the statute in your state.

Due-on-Sale Clauses

If we successfully take over the property by having Terri sign the deed and then we record that deed (to validate our ownership), we may discover that the lender begins foreclosure on us even though we've made up the back payments and penalties!

The reason is that today most mortgages (or trust deeds) contain a "due-on-sale" clause. That means that anytime the title is transferred, the mortgage immediately becomes due. The moment we recorded that deed, it gave the lender constructive notice that a transfer had taken place. At the lender's option, foreclosure to get back the property might commence.

Therefore, before we go through any of this we will want to check with the lender to see that we can safely assume the existing financing. (Sometimes the lender will charge us "points," or a fee, plus a higher interest rate for assumption.)

Some bargain hunters will attempt to circumvent this problem by not recording the deed. The idea is that what the lender doesn't know won't hurt anyone, but this may not be true. Until the deed is recorded, the investor's position in the property is not secure. (Until the deed is recorded, the owner of record is the one on the earlier deed, the original owner. Technically, she can borrow on the property or even sell it again!)

Occupancy Troubles

We might have trouble getting the former owner out, even if we get recorded title on a deed. She might simply refuse to leave. If she contests an eviction suit, she may have grounds (as a former owner) for delaying eviction for weeks, months, or even years.

Conclusion

My personal feeling is that although we can find bargains here, the problems and perils outweigh the benefits. I find these benefits:

1. You get the property at a reduced price.
2. You invest only a few thousand dollars.

But there are these problems:

1. You may have trouble with state laws relating to purchasing property that is in foreclosure.
2. You may have trouble assuming existing financing.
3. You may have trouble with occupancy.

So be careful. There is a bargain here, but it is tricky.

4

Buying Discounted Mortgages in Foreclosure

This is a bargain-hunting method that relatively few people have discovered; hence, it may be ripe for picking. It offers enormous potential rewards with usually manageable risks. It's an area, however, that requires two things to succeed: some expertise and some money.

In the last chapter we looked at profiting from a stage 1 opportunity by buying a property in foreclosure directly from an owner. Here we're also considering investing in a property that's in foreclosure, but this time getting it from a lender.

This may seem a strange place to find a bargain. Why are we concerned with the lender? Isn't the lender the one who's doing the foreclosing?

Yes, and for the lender it can be an experience almost as unpleasant as for the owner—and therein lies the opportunity. Consider this example.

The Reluctant Lender

Henry sells his home. The buyers get a new first mortgage, but they don't have enough for a full cash down payment. So Henry carries back some "paper"; he gives the buyers a second mortgage for some of his equity in the house. The payments are "interest only," meaning that the mortgage balance never gets any lower. Henry just gets paid the interest on it. It's all due and payable in 3 years. The deal looks like this:

Cash down payment	$10,000
Henry's second mortgage	$20,000
First mortgage	$70,000

The buyers pay for 3 years. However, at that time the second mortgage is due. The buyers now owe Henry his full $20,000 in cash. But the buyers don't pay.

The Stonewalling Borrowers

There are no more interest payments coming in, and the buyers don't return Henry's calls when he asks them when they are going to pay off the mortgage. Henry goes to see what the problem is. When he gets to his old house, he's told to get lost and the door is slammed in his face. The current owners won't pay and won't talk.

That second mortgage, which Henry took back at the time of the sale of his property, now looks like a real headache. He is owed the full $20,000, but how does he collect it? Should he foreclose?

What's worse, while he's trying to figure out what to do, he receives notice that the buyers have stopped making payments on the first mortgage as well. The bank, which holds the first, has just filed a notice of default. (Holders of secondary financing usually pay a nominal fee to a service set up at the time of sale that notifies them if the first is in default.) Henry goes to see the broker who handled the sale and is told that if the first forecloses, he could stand to lose all of his $20,000!

The Order of Foreclosure of Mortgages

To understand Henry's dilemma fully, we need to understand how mortgages are prioritized. As those familiar with real estate know, mortgages are numbered in order of their chronology. (This is an easy concept to grasp, but absolutely vital.)

Let's say I loan you $100. You agree to pay me back. Now you go to another friend, Pete, and borrow $50. You also agree to pay Pete back.

Tomorrow you earn $100. Who do you pay back first? Do you pay me? Do you pay Pete? Or do you give a little to each of us?

In real estate these questions could never arise because we would all immediately know who gets paid back first. The rule is: *In foreclosure, the mortgage placed on the property first gets paid back first.* That's why a first mortgage is called a "first," a second mortgage a "second," and so forth. In a forced sale, whatever money is realized from the sale goes first to the first mortgage. Then and only then, if there is anything left, is the second paid, then the third, and so forth down the line. (There is a method, called "subordination," of keeping a loan in a secondary position even if it's chronologically placed first on a property, but that's not germaine here; we'll examine subordination in Chapter 13.)

Henry's Problem

In Henry's case, he holds a second mortgage and the first is foreclosing. If this process were to continue, at the time of the foreclosure sale the property would go to the highest bidder. Naturally the holder of the first would bid the full amount of the first loan, in this case $70,000. If there were no other bids, then the property would be sold to the holder of the first. Henry would get nothing.

Remember the priorities of mortgages: The first money realized goes to the first, and only then does anything left over go to the second and so forth. If only $70,000 were realized (bid by the holder of the first), there would be no money whatsoever left over. Henry's mortgage and any interest in the property would be wiped out.

Protecting the Secondary Lender's Interests

To protect his interests in the property at a foreclosure sale by the first, Henry therefore has to see that the first doesn't foreclose. The only good way to avoid this undesirable eventuality is to get the first mortgage out of foreclosure. To do this, Henry himself would need to quickly make up the back payments on the first mortgage *out of his own pocket.* Once the back payments (and penalties) on the first were made up, the default would be removed and the first would be out of foreclosure. (If Henry's second mortgage is written correctly, it will allow him in this situation to add all payments made on the first mortgage to the second.)

This only ends Henry's immediate problem. The long-term problem, what to do about getting paid on the second, remains. To settle that, he would then have to begin foreclosure on his second, all the while continuing to make up the payments on the first.

The reason Henry would need to foreclose on his second would be to get back his title to the property. Once he had title, then he could try reselling, hoping to recoup his money.

Henry's Foreclosure Does Not Affect the First Mortgage

Note that if Henry forecloses on his second mortgage and the property goes to sale, *the first mortgage is unaffected.* Because of its superior position, the first continues to remain in force. Henry's foreclosure (assuming he is the only one to bid) allows him to gain title to the property and then, hopefully, to resell, subject to the existing first of $70,000, in order to recoup his money.

It's important to be clear about this. If Henry forecloses and gets title to the property, he doesn't eliminate the first. It's still there. He simply secures his own position.

How's Henry Feeling?

Henry is not a savings and loan association; nor is he a mortgage banker or a mortgage broker. He's just a home owner who carried back a second mortgage in order to facilitate the sale of his house. Now, in order to save his money, it appears that he'll suddenly have to put forth additional money and use skills and knowledge he doesn't have. Henry's feeling uncertain, frustrated, and probably not just a little bit scared.

What Henry would like most of all right now is for someone to bail him out. That someone could be you. Let's consider the deal from a bargain hunter's viewpoint.

Is It a Bargain?

In the original sale the buyer's (the current owners) put down $10,000. It's been 3 years. Even with very slow appreciation, if we assume that the property has gone up only 2.5 percent a year, today it's worth about 7 percent more than when it was sold. It's gone from $100,000 to possibly $107,000:

Current owners' equity (includes $7000 appreciation plus $1000 equity return on first mortgage)	$ 18,000
Henry's mortgage	20,000
First mortgage (it's gone down $2000 in 3 years)	68,000
Present worth	$106,000

Note what's happened over the 3 years. The first mortgage has been paid down a little. The house has gone up in value a little. This has turned the current owners' equity from $10,000 into $18,000.

But for one reason or another the current owners don't care about this equity, for they're allowing the property to sink into foreclosure. Similarly, Henry doesn't much care about this equity either. He just wants to get out of the problem the easiest way possible. He just wants to get rid of his headache. But the bargain hunter cares.

The Bargain Opportunity

As the bargain hunter, you can make Henry an offer. Henry already knows that if he forecloses he's going to have to come up with payments and penalties on the first as well as the costs of foreclosing on the second. He also knows that he's going to be moving into foreign territory.

You can relieve Henry's anxiety. You can take away the pain, the frustration, and the work.

But first you must know what it's going to cost you. From the lender of the first you can find out the *exact* payments and penalties. From the trustee you can find out the *exact* costs of foreclosure sale. We'll assume here that these two costs come to $4000.

Once you know the exact costs, you can enter the picture, offering to take that troublesome second off Henry's hands (have it assigned to you). Henry is sure to like that idea. You of course remind him that there are costs and risks involved.

You can point out that Henry's second is now really worth $4000 less, simply because that's the amount he'll have to put out in cash to protect it. Instead of a $20,000 second, in reality he's only got a $16,000 second.

In addition, there are the risks of foreclosing. The current owners might sue or declare bankruptcy or resort to some other tactic, any of which could slow down the foreclosure process. During the whole time the process is delayed, the payments on the first, plus the taxes and insurance on the property, will still have to be paid.

Even if the foreclosure is ultimately successful, there's the chance that the current owners might refuse to leave the property and might fight an eviction suit. This could further delay things.

All of these are, in fact, real risks.

You point out that you will be willing to take on these risks as well as relieve Henry of the burden of the second. You make him two different offers.

Your Offers to Henry

First, you offer him $10,000 in cash. If Henry accepts, he signs the mortgage over to you and he's permanently out of the picture.

Second, as an alternative, you offer to have him sign over the mortgage to you in exchange for a promissory note of $15,000 that bears no interest for 6 months. If by that time you are able to foreclose on the property and *gain title* (and evict the current owners), you'll exchange the promissory note for a fully assumable second mortgage in favor of Henry on the property for $15,000 at a low rate of interest, due and payable in 7 years.

If you can't complete foreclosure in 6 months, then you'll give Henry back his original second, provided he compensates you for any costs you've incurred. If at any time the current owners suddenly have a change of heart and make up the default on the second, you and Henry will split the receipts.

What Will Henry Do?

Both of these offers have appeal to Henry. If he takes your first offer, he gets out free and clear, with no more problem or headache. But instead of $20,000 (the face value of his second), he only receives $10,000. If he takes your second offer, he gets nothing immediately. But if you're successful, in 6 months he gets a second for $15,000 ($5000 more than the cash offer).

The Benefits to You

Under the first offer, you have to put up some $10,000 for a short time to Henry and about $4000 to make good the first mortgage. However, you immediately get the rights to collect on the second. You file a notice of default and start foreclosure.

Once you gain title through foreclosure, you refinance the property. Assume it's worth $106,000 and you get an 80 percent loan, about $85,000. That's enough to recoup all the money you paid Henry and pay off the existing first mortgage of $69,000 plus any additional costs ($3000) you have incurred on the deal. With no net investment, you've just acquired a 20 percent interest in a property!

Under the second offer, the same thing happens. However, you don't have to give Henry the $10,000 up front. Should there be problems and you can't clear the property, Henry is always there to bail you out after 6 months. But if everything goes well, you end up with the same property worth $106,000. With a $69,000 first mortgage plus an assumable $15,000 second (that is, you can sell the property to someone else, who then assumes the mortgage), you thus have an equity of $23,000 for an expenditure of only $4000. Again, not a bad bargain.

Does It Really Work?

In principle, yes. The idea is that we find a lender who is facing foreclosure on a second (or third) mortgage. We examine the property. If there is enough equity to warrant our interest, we make an offer.

Our example here tries to hit a middle ground. Out in the real world, you are likely to find properties which offer a much greater equity as well as those which offer less. The point is that by being willing to take on the foreclosure risk, you can cut yourself in for a handsome piece of the action.

Remember, a novice lender faced with a foreclosure that he or she doesn't want to get involved with is usually very interested in bailing out. Many such lenders will be extremely thankful to any person who offers to take the problem off their hands.

How Do We Find Lenders Like Henry?

One last question remains: Where do we find people like Henry? In the last chapter we talked about the various methods of locating properties that are in default. We then went on to deal with the owner-borrower. In this chapter we are using the same methods. These not only give us the name of the owner-borrower but also that of the lender who is waging foreclosure. This time we just go see the lender.

Hidden Perils

I've already suggested some of these. Although it's unlikely, the borrower could fight back with lawsuits, bankruptcy, partial payments, or other devices to drag out the proceedings. The borrower could refuse to vacate the property.

(*Note:* If the borrower has a change of heart and suddenly pays up, the worst that's likely to happen is that we'll end up with a second for $20,000 for which we paid half. This can be resold to get out our cash and probably a 50 percent profit.)

Other potential problems: There could be other liens on the property that we haven't considered. There could be back taxes.

Also, there's the physical condition of the property. People who allow their homes to go to foreclosure don't usually keep up the yard or the house. There could be physical problems hidden in the property.

Or there could be something else wrong, including problems with the title itself.

Protecting Against the Perils

Can we protect ourselves against these perils? Not entirely. We can get a preliminary title report from a title insurance company. This will probably (but not necessarily) reveal most defects, including other mortgages or liens. It can be a useful guide, depending on how up-to-date it is.

We can try to make a deal with the borrower: "Move out next week and sign a deed to me and I'll give you $500 cash." If this works, we've just avoided the problems of foreclosure and occupancy. (See Chapter 3 for the perils in making such offers.)

We can scrutinize the property and make a guesstimate of its condition. This, of course, could be more difficult if the borrower refuses to let us get inside. Nevertheless, we can usually make a fairly good judgment. (We can also hire structural engineers, builders, etc., to help here.)

Recommendation

At the outset I said that this technique requires some money and some expertise. Yes, it is risky. But after you've done it awhile, as with anything else, you get pretty good at judging the risk.

For the person who has some money and time to invest, this could be a source of bargains. But be prepared to sustain some losses and incur some problems when you first tackle it. And it's a good idea to have a real estate attorney in reserve to handle any legal problems that arise.

5

Buying at Foreclosure Auctions: Big Risks, Big Profits

The glamour area of foreclosures is the auction. Here properties go to the highest bidder. Here, also, some of the biggest buys can be obtained.

In a recent week in the Los Angeles area I saw a condo worth $85,000 go for $42,000, a house worth $235,000 go for $113,000, and a commercial property worth $285,000 go for $127,000. There's no question that the bargains are here.

However, right at the outset it must be understood that this is also the riskiest area of foreclosure to deal with. Many times it involves bidding blind, just hoping that you're doing the right thing. If you don't like taking risks, then you don't belong at foreclosure sales.

Also, it usually involves either having a lot of cash or establishing a strong line of credit from a bank (which is equivalent to having cash). If you don't have money, you don't belong at foreclosure sales, either.

Having thus glimpsed the problems, let's see how to find the benefits.

How a Foreclosure Sale Works

We've already looked at stage 1 of foreclosures (before the sale) in Chapters 3 and 4. Now we're at stage 2, the sale itself.

As noted in Chapter 3, the foreclosure process differs from state to state. For example, let's take the case of California (a good many states are modeled after California). Please keep in mind that the process in other states differs both as to procedure and time. In Texas, for example, the entire process may take only a month! In some parts of New England, there are no trust deeds; instead, true mortgages are used and the foreclosure procedure happens only as part of a court action.

In California, foreclosure normally takes place outside of a court (although court foreclosure is allowed); consequently, the former owner-borrower has *no* right of redemption after the sale. (When court foreclosure occurs, usually the former owner-borrower can redeem the property for a period of time, often a year or more after the sale has taken place.)

After the Default Notice Is Filed

In California, once a notice of default is filed, the owner-borrower has 3 months in which to make up any delinquent mortgage payments and penalties. If these are made up, the mortgage is reinstituted and the parties involved go their way as before.

Once the 3-month reinstatement period has passed, however, things change. Now there is a period of 21 days during which the trustee must *advertise* the property in a newspaper, announcing the coming sale. (This is usually in a legal paper, which often turns out to be a tiny one that few people read.)

During this 21-day period the owner-borrower may redeem the property by paying up all the delinquent payments and penalties and, at the option of the lender, paying back the *entire* amount of the mortgage. Notice that just paying up the back payments and penalties may not be enough.

After this, the trustee sells the house to the highest bidder "on the courthouse steps," which can actually be any public place (such as a courtroom or the trustee's office). The place and time of the sale, however, *must* be announced in the advertisement.

Finding Property to Bid On

To find out which properties are going up for auction, you can simply read the local newspaper in which such auctions are advertised. Alternatively, most counties maintain a service which picks up such notices and which will mail you a list of them. Sometimes, however, the fee for this tends to get a bit heavy.

Finding out about the sales is therefore relatively easy, but locating the property to be sold can be difficult, for only *legal* descriptions are given. As noted in Chapter 3, these do *not* include a street address. It helps to have a friend in a title insurance company who can get you usable addresses from legal descriptions. (See Chapter 3 for other clues on locating the property.)

Once you've gotten the address, you have to take a look at the property, for the public notice does not give its value. You have to determine the property's condition and worth either by using your own judgment or by using expert help. You also need to determine whether there's an occupancy problem.

How to Bid at the Sale

It's elementary. You just show up and bid. Of course, you must have a cashier's check for the maximum amount you plan to bid. (Many times this can be for 10 percent of your bid, with the provision that you'll come up with the balance in a short time.)

You can be sure that the mortgage holder who is foreclosing will be there to bid the full mortgage amount plus back interest and penalties. Thus, at least one other person will be bidding.

In addition, if it's a good property, other bargain hunters may also be present, ready to bid. In some cases the bidding gets fierce and frantic, and it isn't always friendly or entirely on the up and up. (Several bidders may get together to bid up the price until you get disgusted and leave, at which time they withdraw their bids back down to a low price they had earlier agreed upon. There are other nasty tricks as well.)

Nevertheless, in many cases the only other bidder may be the holder of the mortgage, and that person may only bid the mortgage amount. In this case, having no other competition, you just bid slightly more than the mortgage amount—the trustee handling the sale will tell you how much the next highest bid must be—and if the holder of the foreclosing trust deed doesn't want to beat your bid, the property is yours!

If you've done your homework, you may have just doubled your money or more. (There are big risks, of course, which we'll get into shortly.)

The Biggest Pitfall in Bidding at Auctions: Hidden Liens

The single biggest difficulty in dealing with foreclosure auctions is mistaking which mortgage you're bidding on. You could examine the house, determine that it's worth $100,000, and at the sale find out that the mortgage is only $10,000. So you bid $10,100 and are successful. You think you've just bought a house worth $100,000 for $10,100. However, it turns out that there are $90,000 worth of other mortgages on the property, so in reality you've just bought a house worth $100,000 for $100,100—no bargain! (In a foreclosure, remember that if a secondary mortgage is foreclosing, it does not affect the rights of a superior mortgage; thus, when a third forecloses, it does not wipe out the second or the first. See the appendix for a further explanation.)

In most foreclosure auctions there is no way to *guarantee* that there are no hidden mortgages or liens ahead of what you're bidding on.

At the same time, this is not to say that there are *always* other mortgages ahead of the one in foreclosure. Often, a first is foreclosing. A condo with a market value of $75,000, for instance, may have a first mortgage of $42,000 that is foreclosing. The person who bids and buys may get the property for just over $42,000. Now that's a bargain!

Protecting Yourself Against Hidden Liens

Ultimately, there is no way to guarantee that there won't be any hidden mortgages, tax liens, or similar problems on the property. However, you can go a long way toward protecting yourself.

Read the mortgage   This is not as simple as it sounds. Although the mortgage is recorded and a copy is probably available through a title insurance company, you may not know whether the mortgage is a first, second, or third just by examining it. Although in recent years many title insurance companies have taken to writing "this is a secondary lien" right on the face of the mortgage, lest anyone be uncertain, that's not the rule. The mortgage may not specify that it's a second.

An alternative way to find out would be to call the trustee and/or the lender. But can you trust their answers? It would, after all, be to their advantage to have you bidding on what you thought was a first, only to find out later that it was a second.

Search the title   When you need to know the financing on the property, it can be helpful to do a title search.

This can be done fairly quickly, but it can be expensive. If you're a client of a title insurance company, however, a preliminary title search (or "prelim") will sometimes be done for free. The prelim will probably show most liens against the property. An exception is that tax liens or other liens could be recorded *just prior to the sale* and thus not appear in a preliminary report. This is *not* an assured method.

Other Pitfalls

I've already touched on what is probably the worst of these—occupancy. The "tenant" in a foreclosure is usually the former owner-borrower. This person may be quite bitter about what's happened and reluctant to get out. If you buy a property at a foreclosure sale, you may end up with a tenant (the former owner) who won't get out. When you press eviction, the tenant may show up in court with a list of grievances. As noted earlier, I've seen a case in which this cost the bargain hunter tens of thousands of dollars and took nearly a year to resolve.

Of course, there are also the hidden problems, such as broken walls and toilets and stolen fixtures. This is the general damage that an angry borrower might do to the property in a fit of rage before leaving.

Equity of Redemption

Thus far I've been speaking primarily about a mortgage in the form of a trust deed. Some states, however, still use an old-fashioned form of mortgage with a "mortgagor" (lender) and a "mortgagee" (borrower). With this type of instrument there is only judicial foreclosure, that is foreclosure only through court action.

In most cases of judicial foreclosure, there is also "equity of redemption." This means that the former owner-borrower can redeem the property for a set time *after* the sale is completed. (In some states this time is a year or longer.)

In other words, if you are in a state that has only judicial foreclosure and you buy a property through a foreclosure sale, it may be that even after you have title, the former owner has a claim on the property; once having paid back all your foreclosure costs, the person could demand the property. This potential claim could prevent you from reselling, refinancing, or otherwise dealing with the property.

Conclusion

At foreclosure auctions, properties are frequently sold for half or less of their market value. The reasons for this vary. There could be divorce, illness, death, loss of job, or whatever. One would think that in such cases the houses would be put on the market and sold by agents long before they get to foreclosure, but that's not always what happens. Frequently a property will go to foreclosure simply because the former owner can't or won't take the time to handle its liquidation.

Therefore, bargains—very *big* bargains—do exist in this market. They are somewhat offset, however, by the risks. These include the difficulty of determining what other liens may be on the property, the potential problem of occupancy, and the condition of the property.

Recommendation

The most money to be made in foreclosures occurs when we buy at the sale. Unfortunately, the most risk occurs here too.

My advice is that you *must* have expert help to invest here. You should either be an experienced attorney yourself or work closely with a competent one. You should also have lots of extra money to get you over any unforeseen problems. Perhaps most important of all, you must be aware of the risk of buying blind—you might think you're buying a first mortgage when, in reality, it's only a third.

As in most things, when the rewards go up, so do the risks. This is an area for hardy risk takers, those with both money and expertise.

6

REOs: The Most Popular Foreclosures

If you're looking for a foreclosure bargain that's below market, that requires very little down, and that offers the best financing terms in town, then you're looking for an REO.

"REO" stands for "real estate owned." It's a term that banks and savings and loans (S&Ls) use for properties they've taken back through foreclosure. REO means that the lender has become the owner. For banks and S&Ls, it's one of the worst things that can happen.

Why Lenders Don't Want REOs

Lenders don't like REOs. There are many reasons. REOs don't pay interest and lenders are in the business of earning interest. Whenever lenders have money tied up that isn't producing interest, it shows up as a negative factor in their bookkeeping. Too many properties in the REO category can lead to insolvency in a lending institution, and that can lead to its failure. REOs don't look good on the books of a lending institution. They indicate failure rather than success.

Finally, REOs take time and effort away from the lender's main business, making loans.

For these and other reasons, lenders are always anxious to get rid of REOs as quickly as they can. The problem is that in recent years the number of REOs has been increasing. As a result, lenders are under increasing pressure to get rid of those properties quickly. As the pressure on the lenders increases, the better the deals they are willing to offer to buyers. It's a lender's problem, which can be the bargain hunter's opportunity.

A Typical REO

HighInterest Savings and Loan had an REO on its books. It was a three-bedroom, two-bathroom house in a fairly good area of town. HighInterest S&L was hoping in the worst way that it could get rid of that property as an REO. It wanted to be able to convert it from an REO back into a mortgage that paid interest. In other words, it wanted someone to take over the property.

To get rid of the property quickly, the S&L was willing to accept a price of 10 percent below market. (The market was $100,000, and the lender would accept $90,000.) In addition, the S&L was willing to give a buyer a 30-year fixed-rate loan for 2 percent *below* the market interest rate, and that with only $4500 down!

Is it a bargain? As we've indicated before and will see in later chapters, it is probably possible in most situations to get a better price *or* better financing *or* a lower down payment. But what makes this a bargain is that *all three* areas are offered at better-than-normal conditions. As an all-around bargain property, this REO is hard to beat.

Why Lenders Don't Want Anyone to Know They Have REOs

If I've whetted your appetite for REOs, you'll have to hold in the reins for a bit. There's a problem—finding out about them. One would think that as anxious as lenders are to get rid of REOs, they would be out there advertising and promoting them, doing their darndest to get investors to buy them. That's not the case at all.

Banks and S&Ls are very secretive about their REOs. They would prefer that most people don't even know they exist. (Most people don't.) They have three good reasons for keeping REOs quiet.

First, S&Ls and banks are corporations. Like other corporations, they have stockholders. If the stockholders get wind of the fact that the lender has a large backlog of REOs, it's going to erode investor confidence. Some nervous stockholders are going to begin selling stock. When that happens, others may hear of it and a general stock panic could ensue. The stock values could plummet, and that would hurt the lender.

Second, S&Ls and banks depend on their depositors for their funds. Even though most such lenders have federal deposit insurance (not all do, some being state-insured) for up to $100,000 per account, depositors are finicky (particularly those who deposit more than $100,000). The rule seems to be, "If I stick my money in an S&L, I want to be sure it's in good shape even before I worry about the insurance."

If lenders acknowledged that they had a lot of REOs, it might shake depositors' confidence. If depositors started pulling out their deposits, it could start a catastrophic run on the bank. S&L runs have already happened several times since 1981, and both banks and S&Ls are very sensitive and concerned about it.

Finally, announcing a lot of foreclosed property could adversely hurt the retail market. If buyers were aware of what's really out there in REOs, they might cut back on buying regular resales and new houses. This would hurt the lenders' opportunities for making new mortgages.

These are the three very good reasons that S&Ls and banks would like us all to believe that there are few REOs out there. The truth, however, is quite different.

How Many REOs?

Because of the secrecy surrounding REOs, it's impossible to know with any certainty how many are out there. However, it is possible to know how many properties S&Ls and banks foreclose on at any given time. (That's public knowledge to be gleaned from county records.) As of this writing, the best estimate I have heard is that there are something like 300,000 to 400,000 REOs nationwide. That's a lot of properties.

What Kind of Properties Are They?

The vast majority of REOs are houses and condos. Frequently they are in fairly nice areas. A few are in the very best areas . . . or the very worst.

Since most are held by S&Ls (which are the largest lenders on residential real estate) and since S&Ls try to make loans on fairly good property, most of the REOs are very nice. Chances are that you'll find the very best foreclosed properties to be REOs.

Are All REOs a Good Deal?

In many cases they are, although it really depends on what you're looking for. As we've noted, REOs usually combine a little of all the items we look for in a bargain. They are a little below market, the terms are a little better, the down payment is usually a little less, their locations are usually at least adequate, and there are usually no occupancy problems. The combination of all these factors makes them desirable. However, if you want a big price discount or unusually terrific terms or nothing down, you probably won't find these here.

REOs are far better than average deals. They are true bargains. But they usually aren't steals. If you're looking to "steal" a property, then you'd best look elsewhere.

How Do You Find Them?

That, of course, is the trick. With lenders being so secretive about them, you won't find REOs waiting for you to come along. In fact, the most difficult part about this area is finding the properties.

The most logical first step is to check with a lender. Go into your local S&L branch and ask for their REO department. As an experiment while writing this book, I tried that with five different S&Ls. In four cases, the people I talked with had no idea what I was talking about. In the fifth, the person said that she knew, then connected me with their "real estate division." It turned out to be a subsidiary of the S&L that was a residential real estate sales office. They didn't handle REOs at all.

It's pretty hard to get the information from the lender when the lender's own people don't know what's going on!

But of course they do, or at least the manager of the branch does. However, the information isn't going to be given to you just because you walked in the front door off the street. You could, after all, be a reporter doing an exposé on how many REOs this particular S&L had at the time. Or you could just be a blabbermouth.

On the other hand, if you're a depositor (particularly if you have substantial funds deposited) or a stockholder, then the lender's people will feel obliged to talk with you. Usually they'll give you a number, or perhaps even an address which will be the location of that S&L's REO department. (Rest assured, virtually every S&L has an REO department.)

If you're not a stockholder or depositor, you should try to locate the most senior bank employee and convince that person that you really are an investor looking to purchase an REO. You may get lucky. (If you don't get lucky, there are other avenues; we'll be looking into these in a few paragraphs.)

If you are a stockholder or depositor and have flexed your muscles to get to the REO department, or have convinced a branch officer to give you the location or phone number, you may find yourself quite unwelcome once you get there. You may be the very person the lender doesn't want to give the information to for the reasons indicated earlier. Therefore, when you call or show up, the REO officer will probably indicate the following:

1. No list of REOs is available or even exists.
2. No properties are currently being offered for resale to the public. The S&L has its own means of getting rid of any it should happen to repossess.
3. If you leave your name and number, should such a property appear, you will be contacted.

The real story is otherwise:

1. A list of all REOs the S&L holds does exist and is available. It includes the addresses of the properties, their condition, the exact amount the S&L has in them, and their priority for disposal. Even common sense tells us that such a list has to exist, if for no other reason than internal inventorying at the S&L.
2. *All* properties held as REOs are currently being offered for resale. The S&L does indeed have its own means of getting rid of them.
3. You'll be called back the next time the sun freezes over.

What to Do

When you are rebuffed by an REO officer, you know one thing for sure. You're at the right place. The real question now becomes: How do you get the information you want from that person? How do you get to be part of the means of disposing of the properties that the S&L has?

There are at least three answers here.

Contact the Lender's Agent

Ask the REO officer if there is a real estate agent who handles resales for them.

In the past, most S&Ls handled the resale of REOs by themselves. But the volume in recent years has gotten so large that they have taken to working out deals with some of the larger real estate companies. The lenders know that large real estate companies often have investors ready and able to take advantage of bargains. The deal is that the lender will offer REOs to the agents on the condition that the agents don't publicize the fact, but instead dispose of the property quietly to the investors they have ready.

There's nothing illegal or underhanded about this. It's simply a way of getting the properties to market without making a fuss. The REO agent will probably ask where you live. She may then give you the name of an agent near you.

Contact that agent. Explain that you are interested in REOs. Unless the agent has a backlog of investors, he'll probably keep you in mind and you may be contacted the next time an REO hits the market.

Regardless of how many REOs the lender may have, don't expect the agent to be able to offer you more than one or two—and then only on an occasional basis. To keep anyone from knowing how many REOs they really have, S&Ls frequently use many agents and give them only one or two properties at a time. The agents probably only know about the properties in their area. You as a potential investor-buyer will probably only know about one, or maybe two, agents.

Finally, the property you may get in this fashion will probably carry better-than-market terms, but you may end up paying closer to market price. Remember, the S&L has to pay a commission to dispose of property in this fashion.

Make an Appeal Directly to the REO Officer

If done correctly, this is your best chance of getting a good REO deal. Here's how to do it.

First, consider the position of the REO officer. On the one hand, she has all these properties to get rid of. On the other, the lender doesn't want to publicize the fact that the institution has a lot of REOs. Think how you can solve both of the REO officer's problems.

Begin by *not* asking to see the list of REOs. You're not going to get to see it anyway, so there's no sense getting the REO officer agitated.

Next, try the following statement or something like it: "I'm looking to buy an REO in the following price range [name a price range, such as $90,000 to $110,000] in the following area [name an area, such as between Denver and Colorado streets, or on the west side of town, or south of the boulevard in Tarzana]. Do you have any there?"

Consider what you've just *not* asked. You haven't asked if the S&L has a lot of REOs. You haven't asked how many. You haven't asked to see where they are all located.

What you have asked for is a very little bit of information about a specific price range and a specific area. The REO officer isn't going to get fired for telling you that. In fact, if the REO officer tells you, she won't be admitting they have a lot of REOs; she won't be saying where they are. (This solves her problem regarding publicity.) On the other hand, she may be helping to get rid of some of those REOs on the lender's books. (This solves her other problem regarding disposal.)

If you're *ever* going to get an REO officer to tell you about properties, ask for a *specific* price range in a *specific* location.

Typically, the REO officer will now say something like "Yes, we have a couple of properties in the area you are looking at. Here are their addresses. Take a look and see what you think." (If it turns out that the S&L really doesn't have any REOs in the area or price range you've indicated, try changing the area or price.)

You've just reached the next plateau in your REO search.

Find the Property Directly

This bypasses the REO department entirely, at least with regard to locating the properties.

Remember the foreclosure process we discussed in Chapter 5. It involves advertising the sale of the property, then holding a public auction. At that public auction a price is paid and a deed given, which is then recorded. All of this is public information.

In nearly every major metropolitan area of the country today there are publications which record these facts. Sometimes it's called "REO Service," other times "Foreclosure Facts," and so on. For a fee, you can also buy a service which will give much of the following information:

The name of the lender who holds the property

The property's address

The amount paid for the property at the foreclosure sale

The name of the previous owner

The date of the sale

The original loan amount

The year built

The square footage

The property taxes

The assessed land evaluation and the assessed improvement evaluations

These information services aren't inexpensive. They can cost as much as $100 per month, but they will put you in instant touch with REO properties. You can find out about these services from a variety of places. Ask a lender. Check for advertisements in legal or business papers. Check with agents. Look for ads in the yellow pages of phone books.

Once you have the locations of the properties, you can pick ones in specific areas you're interested in and check them out. When you've identified several you like, you can *then* go to see the REO officer.

This time, however, you're coming in with live ammunition in your hand. You already know the property you're interested in. You only have to say, "I understand you own the property at such and such address. I want to make an offer. Let's talk business."

Negotiating Terms with the Lender

Once you've located the property, it's time to make the best deal with the lender. It's important to remember that *everything* is negotiable, depending.

It depends on how desperate the lender is to get rid of the particular property and how much money the lender has in it. (No lender wants to sell for less than the former mortgage amount plus back interest, penalties, and costs.)

If you've found a three-bedroom, two-bathroom dream house in a wonderful area, don't expect the lender to be very anxious to cut the price or terms. You may end up paying close to market price and getting close to market terms. The reason is that if you don't buy it today, it's such a desirable property that the REO officer will feel confident of being able to sell it to another investor tomorrow.

On the other hand, if you're interested in the worst dog the lender has, then you may get it for way below market and the lender may offer financing that's terrific (2 to 4 points below market-rate assumable loans). For those properties in between, you'll get something in between.

Depending on your situation, you can also slant the terms. For example, you may have very little cash. You may make an arrangement whereby you give the lender virtually nothing down in exchange for getting an at-market-rate loan. Or you may put down more cash, say 20 percent, in exchange for a loan at way below the market rate. Or you may pay cash (or get your own other financing) in exchange for a very low price.

Distressed REOs

Even the fixing up of properties in bad condition is negotiable. The REO officer may be aware that the property requires $10,000 in repair work. That may be knocked right off the top of the price. Or the lender may *advance* you the money to make repairs (meaning that once you bought the property, you would be getting additional money paid to you to fix it up). The money advanced could be added to your loan or could simply be an outright direct payment to you from the lender. As I said, it's all negotiable.

How to Get the Best Deal

To get the best deal, first you have to know what you want (price, terms, repairs, etc.) and then you have to find out what is the most the lender will give. As I've noted elsewhere, there are a lot of good books on the market dealing with negotiation. You can try the techniques they offer.

Or you can simply ask. I've found that sometimes it works to just tell the lender what would be the best deal for you. Offer so much down, so much a month, so much as an interest rate, specify the terms, and see what happens. If your offer is realistic, the lender may go along with it or only modify it slightly. In any event, it is a point at which serious negotiations can begin.

Another way to approach negotiation is to ask the REO officer the following questions: "How much will it take to get you out of this property?" "What's the lowest down payment (best interest rate, longest terms, highest repair allowance, etc.) you'll offer me if I take this property off your hands today?"

Once You've Established Contact

Once you've gotten to know the REO officer (after you've purchased your first property), things should move along more smoothly. He or she may offer you a selection of other properties. You might ask to see the "worst dogs" the officer has and may make low-ball offers on them. The possibilities are really endless.

Problems with REOs

The problems with REOs are usually far less than for other repossessed property. Frequently the lender will pay for a policy of title insurance and will guarantee that the loan you get is indeed a first (no hidden liens) and that the title is clear.

You are nevertheless buying a property which you must now take responsibility for. Frequently such sales are "as is." This means that if the property is sliding down a hill and is about to be condemned, it could be your problem. If there's a tenant who won't pay and won't get out, that could be your problem too (although you could negotiate with the REO officer that a condition of your purchase is that the property be vacant when you take ownership). If the property has termites, the lender won't correct the problem.

You must now also rent the property out. You should have done your homework to see that the potential rental income will cover the mortgage payments, taxes, insurance, and other costs.

In other words, the problems with REOs are usually the same as with buying any other investment property. Buying it from a bank or an S&L usually, but not always, means that you're getting a fairly clean deal. Just because a lender is an institution doesn't mean that it's looking out for your interests. You have to keep your eyes open and your mind alert in *all* real estate transactions.

REOs are frequently good bargains for the hunter who doesn't want to work too hard and is satisfied with less than a steal.

7

Buying FHA and VA Repos

Banks and S&Ls aren't the only ones who have taken back repossessed property. The federal government has taken them back as well, primarily through the Veterans Administration (VA) and the Federal Housing Administration (FHA). Their repos can provide opportunities if you're the right kind of bargain hunter.

There are also other federal government repos, including some offered by the Federal Savings and Loan Insurance Corporation (FSLIC), the Small Business Administration (SBA), and some secondary lenders such as the Federal National Mortgage Association (Fannie Mae). However, they are rarely available directly to investors and, as of this writing, are few in number, so we won't go beyond mentioning them here.

I can recall selling FHA and VA repos as a real estate agent back in the 1950s and 1960s. There were quite a few available then. There are many more today.

VA Repos

A VA repo is usually a house (although it could be a condo or duplex) on which the Veterans Administration has guaranteed the financing. It works like this.

Veterans who served on active duty during certain periods of time and who can meet the credit and income qualifications can get a VA mortgage when they purchase a house in which to live. The VA loan offers distinct advantages:

1. A usually lower-than-market interest rate
2. No down payment
3. VA inspection of the house and of the deal to be sure that the veteran isn't being cheated

Because of these benefits, many veterans buy VA. What's important to understand is that the VA doesn't usually fund the money; rather, a regular bank or S&L does. What the VA does is to *guarantee payment.*

If after the purchase the veteran goes into default, the bank or S&L starts foreclosure. However, because of the guarantee, during the foreclosure process the VA steps in and buys the house from the bank or S&L for the mortgage amount plus allowable penalties and costs.

Now the VA owns the house. It usually makes at least a token effort to get payment from the veteran, but that's another story. For our purposes, it's sufficient to understand that the VA now treats this house like an REO, much the same as a bank or S&L would (with a few striking differences, which I will discuss shortly).

The VA doesn't usually release figures on how many repos it has on hand at any time, but most recently it was believed to be in the tens of thousands.

FHA Repos

The FHA works in a similar fashion. One slight difference is that instead of *guaranteeing* the purchase of a home, the FHA *insures* it, but for our purposes this is not important.

As with original VA loans, the FHA insures loans to buyers of homes. However, while only veterans can qualify for a VA loan (that is, a *new* VA loan, since anyone can get a VA repo loan), anyone who can meet the rigorous credit requirements can get an FHA house. There are important benefits to the original buyer:

1. For owner-occupants, there is a very low down payment. (For investors the down payment is about 15 percent as of this writing.)
2. The interest rate fluctuates, but it is generally a little bit lower than market.
3. The FHA inspects and approves the property to be sure that it's in tip-top shape.

4. The FHA loan is fixed-rate and fully assumable, which makes the resale of the house easier.

Like a VA loan, the FHA doesn't usually advance any funds. Rather, it takes out insurance on the loan to protect the lender.

When a buyer defaults, the lending S&L or bank starts foreclosure. In the past the FHA has stepped in, taken over the house, and become the owner. The FHA then treats the property like an REO.

As with the VA program, it's not known exactly how many FHA repos there are, but the number is thought to be in the tens of thousands.

What Motivates the VA and FHA

Both the VA and FHA treat their repos quite differently from the way that banks and S&Ls handle REOs. For one thing, the federal government doesn't have to worry about stockholders or depositors breathing down its neck. Consequently, neither organization seems concerned over publicizing their repos; the FHA frequently takes out large ads in local papers to advertise them.

One thing both agencies are concerned about, however, is being accused of undermining the retail housing market. Because of our free enterprise system and because of the federal government's huge financial position, some people might suggest that the government was exercising unfair advantage if it dumped its repos at a reduced price. The VA and FHA appear to be highly sensitive to any such suggestion and to go out of their way to see that they give no cause for it. Apparently to avoid even the hint that they might be competing unfairly with private business, both the VA and FHA strive to offer their repos at market level prices. You usually won't find any below-market steals on these properties.

The VA and FHA Disposal System

The government disposal system is aimed at getting the houses back into the hands of owner-occupants. Therefore, both agencies normally spend considerable time and money cleaning and fixing up their properties before offering them for sale. You can frequently tell a VA or FHA repo by the fact that it's one of the nicest-looking houses on the block. The windows have been repaired and cleaned, the house has been painted inside and out, the appliances are in working condition, the flooring has been fixed, and so on. Although the yards aren't usually in such great shape, the houses have generally been put back into like-new condition.

Then the properties are offered for sale. The terms are usually similar to the following:

1. Current market price, based on an appraiser's report.
2. VA or FHA financing to buyers (although you don't have to be a veteran to get a VA loan).
3. You must intend to *occupy* the property to get VA financing. (With FHA, you can be an investor *if* you put more down, currently 15 percent.)
4. The properties offered for sale are usually advertised, and normally any broker in the area can handle the sale. (The VA and FHA both pay commissions to agents.)

Where's the Bargain?

The bargain hunter can find some advantages here. For one thing, the property being purchased is in good condition, probably better than most any other resale around. For another, the FHA and VA financing is highly desirable because it makes resale much easier. (Remember, the loans are fully assumable.)

On the negative side, the buyer must either intend to live in the property or pay a higher down payment if it's going to be an investment.

Then there's the matter of the price. I believe that both the VA and FHA do strive to price their properties as close to market value as possible. However, strange things do happen.

Recently I observed two different FHA repos. In one case the price of the property was $110,000. It was offered for sale and a date was given for submitting offers. No offers were submitted. The problem was that the market values for similar houses in the area were at least $25,000 lower. The FHA placed the house back on the market at $90,000. Again no offers were received. It was finally able to sell the property for $87,000, which was pretty close to market value.

In the other instance the FHA put a house on the market for $112,000. The market values for similar properties, however, were closer to $125,000. Because of an appraisal goof, this house was a real bargain.

However, that doesn't mean that a bargain is necessarily easy to come by. There were dozens of offers on the latter property. (It didn't take a genius to add up the figures here, and with the advertising and exposure there were lots of investors who knew about it.)

I happened to know the agent who handled the successful bidder. Her offer happened to be $118,000. Yes, that's right, she offered $6000 *more* than the asking price! There were other offers higher than the asking price, but hers was the highest. She got the house at what was still a below-market price, plus she had the advantage of a cleaned up property and government financing.

Where to Find FHA and VA Repos

These are the easiest of all repossessions to locate. Just go into any active broker's office and ask them about the properties. They will either have a list to show you or, if they don't handle them personally, be able to recommend another broker who does.

Your broker can usually get a key so that you can inspect the property.

Special Circumstances

I have seen a few houses that have been disposed of differently than I've just described. These properties often had special circumstances (this is particularly true with FHA). The cases I've seen involved extensive damage to the property. Typically, the damage is something that isn't easily corrected, such as a property which is on unstable soil and which has already been partly damaged by a landslide. A building contractor's estimate of the repair costs, when added to the original mortgage amount plus repossession costs, frequently exceeds the market value of such property. Hence, it makes little sense for the government agency to fix up the property and try to resell it. In this case the house may be sold as is.

"As is" government repos are usually sold for substantially below market price. I have seen them offered for as little as a third of what a comparable house in good condition would go for. However, they are typically sold for cash. No FHA or VA financing is available.

These houses are a big risk. They are usually fixer uppers of the worst kind. However, if that is your cup of tea, then there might be opportunities here. To find them, you just have to find a broker who will work with you and keep you informed of government repos. These special cases are few and far between, but they do occasionally show up. (See Chapter 9, "Distressed Properties," for additional clues.)

The Bottom Line

Should you look for an FHA or VA repo?

If you're a bargain hunter, the answer will really depend on your escape plan (discussed in Chapter 1) and your situation. Remember, in most circumstances you are required to occupy (live in) the property.

I have, however, seen some bargain hunters who had cash, put down the 15 percent required on an FHA repo, and then rented it. If they got a reasonably good price, they figured they were way ahead of buying anything else on the market. After all, the house had these advantages:

1. It was in good shape.
2. They didn't have an occupancy problem. (Check current VA and FHA policies regarding occupancy on repos here.)
3. They had a good loan at or below market rate which could be assumed by someone else, making later resale easier.

There's no use thinking that a government repo is going to be a steal. It's not. If you want that, look at some of the other bargains I discuss. But for the right investor, it could be a sound property to consider.

8

Private REOs

Thus far we've considered REOs that were owned by lenders such as S&Ls or by government agencies such as the VA or FHA (properties more properly called repos). Now let's consider one last category which most bargain hunters completely overlook. I call it "private REOs."

A Private Headache

There are many individuals who get involved in real estate repossessions unexpectedly and in an unwanted fashion. For example, Fred took back a second mortgage for $10,000 on his house 3 years ago. He thought he was through with the property.

But when it came time for the buyer to pay off the balloon on the second, the person defaulted. Fred was forced to start foreclosure proceedings and *take back* the property. Now Fred's got a real headache.

During those 3 years the former owner had rented the property out. The tenants didn't take care of it and now it's a mess. The carpeting is ruined. There are holes in the walls. The toilet bowl is cracked. The house needs paint inside and out.

What's worse, since Fred originally sold the property, he has moved. Now he lives 300 miles away. He can't be there to do the work himself or even to have someone else supervise it. The final straw is that he's now making payments on an empty house.

Fred doesn't want to be a real estate landlord with the headaches involved. He doesn't want to own property far away from where he lives. So he's thinking about how to get rid of it.

Fred's Eventual Solution

His logical answer, as soon as he thinks it through, will probably be to list the property with a local agent. He will hope to sell the problem away.

However, there are going to be problems selling a distressed house. The agent will undoubtedly first inform him what the price would be *if* the property were in tip-top shape. But the price will have to be reduced by the amount required to fix up the place—plus an additional reduction to cover the liability of showing a distressed property in order to get a sale. The price a house can get is in part determined by how well it "shows" to prospective buyers. A distressed house shows badly; hence, the price has to be lowered to compensate for this fact.

The Figures Speak for Themselves

Fred originally sold the property for $100,000 and got $15,000 down from the buyer. Since then, properties have gone up by perhaps $5000 in the area. Thus, he theoretically has a $20,000 equity after repossession.

However, there's the deduction for fixing up the house, the deduction for the way it shows, and the cost of the agent's commission (about $6300 if it's 6 percent). Fred realizes that he'll probably make a few bucks *if* he sells it right away. On the other hand, every month that drags by means he's making payments on the first mortgage ($800 per month) plus payments for taxes, insurance, and utilities.

What Fred Would Really Like to Do

Fred would really like to junk the property. If someone would take it off his hands, he'd probably be willing to let it go for just what he has in it (the $10,000 second mortgage plus his costs of repossession). Fred is a bargain opportunity for the asking.

Finding the Bargain

Fred's house offers the bargain hunter an opportunity to do Fred a favor while at the same time picking up a substantial equity with little or no money down. The essence of making it work, however, is locating Fred *before* he lists the house.

Finding people like Fred is the same as finding REOs. It's a matter of checking to see what properties are sold in foreclosure sales and then of contacting the lenders who foreclosed. Most will be S&Ls, but among the bunch will be a few Freds.

Taking Advantage of the Bargain

There are several ways that a bargain hunter could structure a purchase of Fred's property. Here are two.

Plan 1

Offer to pay Fred in cash for all his costs of foreclosure (probably a few thousand dollars) *if* he will give you title to the property and a new second trust deed for the original $10,000.

This isn't a bad offer, although it doesn't entirely get rid of the property for Fred. It pays him back his out-of-pocket expenses. And he hasn't lost a dime, because the same second is back on the house. The only danger to him is that you won't pay when the second comes due and he'll have to foreclose and go through the whole hassle again. But that's a maybe sometime in the future, and you're promising to remove his headache right now.

Plan 2

Offer to pay Fred in cash for all his costs of foreclosure, and also give him $7000 in cash for his $10,000 second.

Not a bad offer. Fred gets his foreclosure costs back plus $7000 in cash. And he gets to walk away from the house. Considering the problems involved, it's a quick solution that Fred just might take.

How much does plan 2 cost you? Nothing!

You write the deal so that you can paint and fix up the house in escrow before the sale. Once you've fixed the house up, you refinance it as part of the transaction. Your new loan is 80 percent of the market value:

Market value (after cosmetic repairs)	$105,000
Loan percentage (80%)	× 0.8
Loan amount you get	$84,000

You get about $84,000 from the refinancing and spend it in this fashion:

Pay off original first (it's gone down $2000 during the 3 years since Fred originally sold)	$68,000
Pay off Fred ($7000 for second plus $3000 for foreclosure costs)	10,000
Cosmetic repairs to property	3,500
Costs of purchase (loan points, etc.)	1,500
Total costs	$83,000
In your pocket after deal closes!	$ 1,000

Refinancing allows you to acquire the property with an equity of $20,000 and at the same time puts $1000 in cash back in your pocket. Now that's a bargain!

Can You Do It?

All it takes is finding someone with a problem like Fred's. I can assure you that such people are everywhere around us. For Fred the property was the worst kind of headache. For you it can be one of the best bargains.

Perils

Be sure you get title insurance on the property and handle the sale through an escrow. Don't trust Fred. He might not be honest and could add a lien to the property without telling you.

Also, as always, check for problems of occupancy.

Finally, be sure you know what repair problems are required and that you can handle them. (See Chapter 9.)

Conclusion

Private REOs are great when you can find them. But I would be less than honest to say that they are easy to find or that you're going to be able to run into them every day. These properties take hard work, lots of it. But there are bargains to be had.

9

Distressed Properties

"Distressed property" means any kind of real estate which has been neglected, abused, or otherwise damaged. It could simply mean a house that needs paint, carpeting, and other cosmetic repair work (commonly called a fixer-upper), or it could refer to a property that has been flattened by a tornado. The whole point is that the damage done reduces the price—means a potential bargain.

Most people think of distressed property as "cheap." It can indeed be inexpensive property, but it can also be top of the line. For example, a friend recently bought a house in the Pacific Palisades section of Los Angeles. The house had originally been appraised at $1.3 million, but an earthquake had triggered a landslide, which had severely damaged the property. My friend bought it for $430,000. He then spent another $250,000 pumping a special adhesive mixture into the soil to stabilize it and another $150,000 fixing up the house. His total expenses over 6 months were about $850,000. He sold for $1.2 million, netting a profit of $350,000. That was an expensive distressed property bargain!

Not All Distressed Property Is a Bargain

Not all properties that are damaged, however, are bargains. I once remember looking at a house that appeared normal in every way from the front. Walking through to the back, however, I found that a steep landslide had erased the backyard and much of the back of the house.

The property was in an area of $90,000 homes and the owner was willing to sell for only $45,000—half price. I decided, however, that the property wasn't worth 10 cents, let alone the asking price. The reason was that the landslide had made the lot virtually useless. Even if the present structure were torn down, it is doubtful that it would ever make economic sense to build any other structure there. This was a case not of a distressed but of a deceased property!

The Three Elements of a Bargain Distressed Property

In order for a distressed property to make economic sense for the bargain hunter, it must not only meet the seven criteria discussed in Chapter 2 for *any* bargain property. It must also meet the following three criteria:

1. Damage that reduces the price
2. Repairability
3. A true profit margin

The first two are fairly obvious. Without damage, the price wouldn't be reduced; therefore, in this type of bargain we are hoping to find damage that ranges from the simplest cosmetic problems (such as lack of paint) to the most severe structural problems. Damage indicates the possibility of a bargain.

The second element is that, whatever the damage, we must have a successful plan for repairing it. This is the key to dealing with distressed properties. Some enterprising bargain hunters make their fortunes by buying property which everyone else is afraid to touch. They succeed because they have a plan for making repairs. A lot of experience and knowledge are necessary here.

The third element is the one that new bargain hunters in the distressed property field most often overlook. Yet it must be considered before any purchase is made.

The True Profit Margin

The true profit margin (TPM) is the profit that we can expect to make. We determine it by first figuring out how much the repairs are going to cost us and then calculating the margin between our purchase price and the actual market value. Let's take a simple example.

Fran found a house that she felt might be a bargain. It was in a terrible state of disrepair. It had been a rental for years and the tenants had torn it apart. In addition, the house was about 25 years old and desperately needed a new driveway and roof. As she walked through the house, Fran carefully made a list of all the things that needed repairing.

She then contacted different tradespeople and got estimates for how much it would cost to have the work done. (After you've worked distressed properties for awhile, you'll get to know these costs automatically.) She added up the costs:

Paint	$1000
Carpeting	2500
Roof	3500
New driveway	1200
Landscaping	300
Total cost of repairs	$8500

Fran knew that a similar house in tip-top shape would sell for around $90,000. The owner here was asking $80,000 but had indicated that a lower offer might be acceptable.

Fran decided to offer $75,000. If the owner accepted, she would be getting the property for $15,000 below market. She would then fix it up for $8500, leaving her a profit margin of $6500. She considered this to be a good bargain.

Was it?

Not really. Fran hadn't considered the TPM. To find the TPM, we must subtract the true costs from the market value:

Market value	$90,000
True costs	
Cost of repairs	8,500
Liquidation (estimated)	7,500
Total	$16,000
Maximum price to pay	$74,000

Thus, to break even on the deal (zero margin), Fran would need to purchase the property for no more than $74,000. To make a profit, she would need to buy for less. In other words, buying for $75,000 was simply not cheap enough. Her costs exceeded her margin, and hence there was no profit; there was a potential loss of $1000.

Are the Expenses Realistic?

I am frequently asked if expense figures such as I've quoted here are truly realistic when one is dealing with a distressed property. For example, what if Fran did much of the repair work herself and saved half the cost of the repairs? What if she sold the house "by owner" and saved the commission (probably $5000 or more)? Couldn't she turn a profit by doing these things herself?

My answer is that if you're going to be a serious bargain hunter, then no, you can't count on turning a loss into a profit by doing the work yourself. Here's why.

You Must Pay Yourself a Salary

Regardless of who does the work, it costs money for labor. If Fran paints, fixes roofs and driveways, and installs carpeting, then the time she spends doing this work is time she can't spend at some other job. In other words, Fran has to pay herself a salary, regardless. Maybe she's unemployed and this is a way of putting herself to work for a month or more. There's nothing wrong with that as long as she and we don't confuse working for a salary with making a profit on a property.

Safety Calls for Calculating Liquidation Costs

With regard to the commission and other liquidation costs, I know that some people don't worry about it. They just figure that God will provide a buyer when needed. I don't work that way. To be safe, I feel that one has to be able to count on selling the property without a loss as soon as it's fixed up. You may need the cash, you may not be able to rent it, you may become ill and need to get out of the business, or any of a hundred other things could happen; therefore, a quick liquidation should be part of everyone's escape plan (see Chapter 1). Quick liquidations mean paying commissions and other costs. Hence, these costs must be factored in.

Now let's take some examples of successful distressed property bargains.

The High-Class Distressed Property

I mentioned in Chapter 1 that bargain hunters eventually develop a style, a particular kind and location of property that they look for. At the beginning of this chapter we saw one bargain hunter whose style is top-of-the-line distressed property. Now we'll consider another and look into the reasons she prefers high-priced properties.

Jane prefers properties in the $300,000 to $500,000 price range. One time, driving out to look at such a property she was considering in Beverly Hills, I asked why she specialized in such expensive investments.

"Because the TPM is so great," she said. "Suppose I buy a house that's worth $100,000 for half price. Now say that I have to stick a quarter of its value into repairs. I've thus paid $50,000, and added $25,000 in repairs, making my total investment $75,000. If I now sell for $100,000, I clear $25,000, out of which I may pay as much as $10,000 in commission and closing costs. My eventual profit might only be $15,000.

"On the other hand, suppose I buy a house which will have a market value of $400,000 after I fix it up. I buy for half price, stick the same quarter of its value into repairs, and end up with a $300,000 investment. Now I sell for $400,000 and clear $100,000. Even after taking the commission and closing costs out of this $100,000, I've now got a handsome profit, perhaps enough so that I only need to find one such deal a year." I persisted and asked her how she could buy a house with a market value of $400,000 for half price. "I don't," she said. "I buy it for less!"

Turning Severe Damage into Profit

As we proceeded onto the property, Jane explained her secret. The house was on a hillside, as are many of the homes in Beverly Hills. Water runoff had eroded the hill under the house. Part of it was still firmly anchored on its hillside lot, but part, where the land had washed away, was hanging exposed over empty air. The foundation had cracked and fallen away, and that area of the home had slanted precariously downward. Needless to say, the property had been condemned by the city.

"Now that's a distressed house," I said.

"Exactly," Jane nodded. She proceeded to tell me what the present owners had told her. At least half the house would need to be demolished. Then the ground would have to be filled in and packed. Finally, a new structure would have to be built.

"Sounds expensive," I commented. "About $235,000," she said, if it's done their way. Instead, I plan to sink three prestressed concrete piers into the soil just beyond the side of the house where the ground has washed away. Then I'll use steel on the piers to form a solid wall, put solid beams under the house, jack it up onto this new foundation, fix any small cracks cosmetically, landscape, and it's done—at $50,000 tops.

"But why don't the present owners do that?"

"They haven't thought of it," she said. "And if they did, they'd probably think the idea was too outlandish to consider seriously."

"So what you're saying is that you'll get the current owners to knock $235,000 off the market value because of the repair work they think is necessary. Then you'll come in and do the work for only $50,000, pocketing the difference of $185,000."

Market value	$400,000
Less estimated cost of repairs	235,000
Owners' reduced price	$165,000
Plus actual cost of repairs	50,000
Total cost	$215,000
Difference (market value less cost)	$185,000

She nodded, then went on to explain the keys to making the deal work: "I have to find property where the problem is severe. I have to be willing to be innovative and to take a chance. That's my risk. The owners have to be convinced that they can't get a better price."

The Secret to Finding the Right Property

One final point: I asked Jane how she was able to locate properties like the one we had seen. "The real secret," she said, "is that the property has to be bad enough that a lender won't give the present owner or some other buyer a new loan. If they can't refinance, then they can't get the money to fix it up themselves and they have to sell."

I asked Jane if that meant she had to have a lot of cash.

"Yes, I work with cash. But I usually give the owner very little cash for the property—just a mortgage for a short term, say a year, for the equity. When I fix up the property and sell, then I pay off the mortgage."

"I need cash, however, to make the repairs. What I've done is put together a little syndicate of investors. They put up the cash in exchange for a share of the profits. That way I raise the entire $50,000 I need for repairs without having to put up a dime of my own money."

I asked if she didn't have to give the investors some of the profit. "Sure," she said, "but these deals are so fat that there's enough to go around and make everyone happy!"

Jane's style was to work with high-priced properties that had big problems. Not everyone, however, likes to work that way.

The Mid-Priced Distressed Property

Alice's style was to look for bargains in mid-priced property. She preferred standard three-bedroom, two-bathroom homes in blue-collar neighborhoods. This usually meant a market value in the $80,000 to $100,000 range in her area.

I went out with Alice to look at one of her "gems in the rough," as she called them. She referred to her properties as her jewelry.

The house was about 25 years old and located on a fairly heavily traveled street. The location was average—no big pluses or minuses.

From the outside the house was obviously in desperate need of repairs. The moment we entered our noses curled up. The property had been rented out and the previous tenants had kept dogs locked inside. The animals had urinated and defecated throughout the house. The smell was horrendous.

As we made our way through the rooms, I noted that the carpet was badly soiled and stained. The walls needed painting and in various places had holes knocked through them. Several doors were missing, and the glass was broken out of the back windows. The kitchen stove was torn apart, and pieces of it were lying about the room. The house had two bathrooms, and both toilet bowls were cracked. One sink had been torn from the wall.

"It's hard to imagine why anyone would do this to a house," Alice commented. I nodded. We had both seen similar damage before.

The backyard was overgrown with weeds, but the real problem was revealed when we looked at the roofline. The timbers holding the roof to the house had buckled for some reason. The result was that the roof had lifted off the house by almost 2 inches at the center. It appeared to be severe structural damage. Alice only smiled. "That's what I was hoping for," she said.

Analyzing the Damage

As we drove back, she explained: "If the house were in perfect condition, it would be worth about $95,000. However, in its present condition I intend to offer the owner $70,000. I think he might accept for three reasons.

"First, I've investigated and found out that the owner's mortgage is only $60,000, so he has enough equity to sell for what I'm offering. Some properties," she added, "are mortgaged for more than they are worth, so the owners can't sell even if they want to.

"Second, the current damage—and particularly the smell—make the house's appearance so bad that it's unlikely anyone would rent it or that most people would even consider buying it. Thus, the property is a big headache for the owner.

"Third, regardless of how bad it may appear, all of the damage to the property, except for the roof, is cosmetic. I know it, and furthermore so does anyone who's ever worked distressed property. And the owner probably knows it.

"That's why the raised roofline in the back is so important. It indicates severe structural problems. Nine out of ten investors wouldn't touch it. Because of that raised roofline, the owner will be forced to take much less in price."

The Repairs

I asked Alice what she intended to do with the property once she got it. "I'll have it painted inside and out," she said, "have new fixtures installed, have the carpets cleaned, and rent it. I've done it before, and I figure that the total cost will be about $5000. That will still leave me with a $20,000 equity."

"But what about the raised roofline?" I asked. "What do you plan to do about that?"

"Basically nothing. The house is 25 years old. If the roofline has risen 2 inches in that period of time, I'm not worried. The worst it's likely to do is to rise another 2 inches in the next 25 years. While I'm having the house fixed up, I'll have somebody nail a covering board over the exposed area so that water doesn't get in. I'll probably get it done for under $20."

"You're just going to cover it up?"

Alice looked offended. "Certainly not. It would be immoral and illegal not to mention the problem to the next buyer. I'll point out that I've sealed the area so that moisture can't get in, and I'll explain exactly my reasoning—that it's a problem, but that the likelihood of it getting worse isn't that bad. If the roof doesn't leak and it doesn't look bad, who cares?"

The Secret of Her Success

"The real secret in these mid-priced properties," Alice said, "is to find some defect that most people, including the owner, agree is horrible. That becomes a price dropper. What's crucial, of course, is for *me* to know that this horrible problem is either readily correctable or something that I can live with indefinitely."

The Lower-Priced Distressed Property

Like Alice, most people are looking for the average house in the average location. But some people find bargains at the bottom of the barrel.

Larry was a bargain hunter who searched for properties in what was a lower economic section of town. Most of the houses here were older and less expensive.

"My escape plan doesn't include selling," Larry confided as we drove out to look at a house he was considering. " I'm in strictly for the long run. My goal is to buy, fix up, and rent. I already own 12 properties, and within a year I hope to have 20."

Saying that this was admirable, I then asked what advantage he was particularly looking for in a distressed house. By now we had driven up to the subject property. It was on a quiet street of older and smaller homes. Most, but not all, of the surrounding houses were fairly well kept up.

The subject house, however, was in great disrepair. The front yard was all weeds. As we moved through the house, we could see that it needed painting badly. However, it wasn't in as bad shape as Alice's house had been. The kitchen and the single bathroom were generally in sound condition, as was the roof. It could probably have used a new driveway.

The Advantage of Lower-Priced Property

"These houses sell for about $55,000," Larry said. "I look at five or six a week. I'll make a lowball offer on this one of about $45,000. I may have to make a dozen such offers, but sooner or later someone accepts.

"Basically, I buy for no down payment. I assume the existing financing and give the owner a mortgage for his or her equity. The mortgage is for 15 years and is fully amortized. Eventually it gets paid off.

"The house looks a lot worse than it is. I have a crew of college kids who'll come in and fix the yard, clean up, paint, and even lay carpet. For about $2000 I can have this house in presentable shape so that I can rent it for top dollar for the area."

Larry's Secret: The Price-to-Rent Ratio

"The key to it all for me," said Larry, "is to buy the properties cheaply enough. If I buy cheaply enough, then the money I get in for rents will cover all my expenses. I'll have a positive cash flow.

"The reason this works out is that rents everywhere have been going up over the past 5 years. Higher-priced houses, however, are still much too expensive in most cases for you to be able to rent them for your payments. Low priced houses are different. There, you can frequently rent for more than the payments.

"Take this house, for example. If my offer is accepted, I'll have bought it for $45,000 with no cash out of my pocket. (Of course, I'll spend $2000 fixing it up.) My payments including everything, will be about $500 a month, yet I can rent it easily for about $525. That puts a positive cash flow of $25 per month into my pocket.

"In addition, I start off with $10,000 equity in the property, and that builds. And of course there are the tax advantages. Finally, I can eventually raise rents and improve my cash flow picture enormously."

The No-Liquidation Escape Plan

I pointed out that if he had to liquidate, he wouldn't have much profit at all.

"Of course you're right," he said. "But my escape plan only calls for liquidation in an emergency. I buy at least $10,000 below market. If I have to sell, even adding my costs of fixing up, I can get out without being hurt. I won't make a profit, but I won't lose either."

"On the other hand, I'm not buying to sell. I'm buying to keep and hold. Since I buy so low, I can get property that I can rent out and make a positive cash flow on."

Larry's price-to-rent ratio was a minimum of 1 percent. He would only buy a property if he could rent it for at least 1 percent of the purchase price. The higher the ratio, of course, the better. That meant that a property that cost him $45,000 had to be rentable for at least $450 per month. (In this case it was $525, considerably better—a 1.2 percent ratio.)

Commercial Opportunities

Thus far we have only considered distressed homes. But all kinds of property can fit this category: for example, commercial property.

I recently looked at a piece of commercial real estate that was truly distressed. It was a fairly large lot, zoned commercial. In the front of the lot was a closed, broken-down hamburger stand needing repairs. At the back of the lot was a do-it-yourself car wash. In the middle was a garage for the storage of cars. The only part of the property that was currently bringing in income was the storage garage.

I didn't want this property for myself (for reasons I'll discuss shortly). But a friend, George, whose style was commercial property, was thrilled by it.

We estimated the value of the lot to be $75,000. The value of the hamburger stand and car wash could only be estimated on the basis of the net income they could produce. George estimated that in good working condition they would bring in a combined $1000 per month, or $12,000 per year. Using a gross multiplier of 8 as a guesstimate (see the section "Terms" in Chapter 2 for an explanation of such multipliers), he estimated their worth at about $96,000. The garage was bringing in $300 per month, or $3600 per year, so he guessed its value to be about $29,000.

Lot alone	$ 75,000
Hamburger stand and car wash	96,000
Garage	29,000
Commercial property value	$125,000

Calculating the Bargain

"I'll offer the owner $85,000," George said. "I've already checked the financing and that's about what he owes. In other words, I'll take it off his hands. Of course, he may counter, but I'm willing to pay up to $90,000 for the property.

"An income property's value is based on the income it produces," he noted. "In this case, it's got almost no income. Apparently the owner isn't able to get it up and running so it can produce income; hence, he must already be expecting to sell for a loss. He has a headache here, one I can cure for him."

I asked George how he was figuring the deal.

"Easy," he said. "The hamburger stand probably cost only $20,000 to build brand new. I'll spend $5000 and have it in tip-top shape. Another $2000 will put the car wash back in business. I'll lease both out and collect the rents.

"Once everything is back in operation, I'll have a property worth $125,000 that I bought for at least 25 percent off. I can hold it for rental income or sell it for profit. That's what I call a bargain."

Getting Out of Your Style

I left George blissfully pondering what he would call his new hamburger stand. (He ended up calling it "Gorilla George's Gourmet Burgers.") For him, it was indeed a bargain. But it wasn't for me, and it may not have been for you.

The reason has to do with style. My own style with regard to distressed property involves residential real estate. I feel comfortable there. I know I can rent it out, and I know what I need to do to get the property in shape to attract tenants.

On the other hand, I don't know anything about the car wash business or the restaurant business. Yes, I might be able to find a tenant to lease out these businesses. But I really don't know what I need to do to fix the property up to attract that tenant. And here (in contrast to my residential properties) I don't know a good tenant from a bad one. My point is that in this case the distressed bargain was only a bargain for the right person—for the one whose style involved commercial property. George immediately knew what to do and how to do it. I didn't.

What's more, I had no desire to learn. I liked my style and wanted to stick with it.

Location Bargains

The final distressed property bargains we'll consider are location bargains. This is stretching our definition of a distressed property a bit, but I think it'll be worth it.

Donna liked location bargains. Recently she took me out to see her latest purchase. We drove to a fancy neighborhood. It had big new houses interspersed with older and much smaller homes.

"This is a jumbled neighborhood," she said. "Big new houses in the $300,000 price range mixed with little old houses selling in the $150,000 price range." We drove up to her new purchase. It was a little old house. "If this house were anywhere else in town, it would probably sell for $75,000. But in this neighborhood I paid $145,000 for it.

"What I'm going to do is to refurbish and add on to it. I'll probably spend $75,000 adding a new master bedroom, a kitchen, and a large family room. When it's finished, the house will look like one of the big houses in this neighborhood. I'll put it up for sale for $300,000 and make $75,000 profit before liquidation costs."

I mention Donna's style only because quite a few bargain hunters are using it. Looking for jumbled neighborhoods in which the smaller houses are really location bargains can pay off. The technique, however, usually requires a fair amount of cash to pull off.

The Bottom Line

Some people worry that there aren't distressed property bargains out there. They lament that these properties get scooped up as fast as they come on the market.

It isn't necessarily so. Some properties have severe problems and stay on the market for months waiting for the right person with a solution. New ones are coming up for sale constantly.

There are still distressed properties out there, lots of them. You just have to look carefully. Also, be sure that you really do have the experience and knowledge to pull off the solution you have in mind.

10

Probate, Tax Auctions, and Other Forced Sales

For those who like a challenge, bargain opportunities abound in a wide variety of forced sales. Here it is frequently possible to purchase a property for a fraction of its market value. The beauty of these sales is that they are held frequently in many communities around the country. If you want to look for bargains in forced sales, chances are that one is being held somewhere near you this week.

While most forced sales involve cash, this is not always the case. Frequently the property being disposed of will be subject to existing mortgages, which in essence means that you only need the down payment. In many cases it is possible to arrange outside financing in advance for 80 percent or more of the purchase price. (Check into Chapter 14 to see how to raise 100 percent of the financing.)

What Are Forced Sales?

A forced sale is essentially a liquidation. For one reason or another a property owner wants to cash out. That property is therefore put on the auction block and goes to the highest bidder.

Properties at forced sales almost always sell for less than market value, sometimes considerably less. There's a good reason for this.

Consider a home buyer looking to purchase a house. The buyer probably contacts a number of agents and goes to see the houses listed. The houses are open for inspection. Often they have been prettied up.

When the buyer selects one to purchase, the purchase is handled in a civilized fashion. An offer is made and negotiations commence. One or more agents work with the buyer to consummate the deal. Soon a deal may be struck. Once the papers are signed, the buyer knows the house is tied up. Assuming the deal was properly worded, the buyer usually has 30 to 90 days to secure financing; if proper financing can't be obtained, the buyer can back out without losing a dime.

On the other hand, consider the case of a forced sale. Inspecting the property may be difficult. It may be necessary to call up an executor or administrator and get that person to take time off from work to come out and show the property, which may prove to be neglected and in disrepair.

A buyer who wishes to purchase it must then usually show up before a judge or magistrate and publicly bid for the property with other buyers. Often the buyer must immediately come up with a 5 or 10 percent cash deposit. Instead of a long escrow, anywhere from no time at all to 20 days may be allowed to raise the full price—in cash. And if the buyer can't find proper financing, however earnestly having sought it, then he or she may lose the entire deposit!

As a result, few people are inclined to become involved in forced sales. Very rarely will a home buyer bid. And because of the hassle involved, relatively few investors bid either. Consequently, the only people who usually show up are bargain hunters. And they, as we all know, aren't going to be willing to pay anywhere near market price. Hence, properties that sell at forced sales usually go for below market—sometimes far below market. There are bargains to be had here.

A variety of forced sales are available. Principle among these are probate sales, tax sales, and consigned auctions. Each is handled a bit differently than the others.

Probate Sales

Probate is the American way of disposing of property upon an individual's death. It arises out of British common law and in theory its purpose is designed to see that all interested parties have the opportunity to present their lawful claims and have them paid from the dead person's estate.

In practice, what this means is that probate allows all creditors to be paid off. In essence, therefore, probate is the legal means that creditors have of collecting debts after a person dies.

The problems and drawbacks of probate are legend. Anyone who has ever been an heir and seen the deceased's estate scooped out to pay creditors, enormous probate attorney fees, and other costs must surely dread the whole process. (There are several ways of avoiding probate, including living trusts and changing the way that title to property is held, and you'd do well to check with your attorney.)

Because of the need to raise cash to pay off creditors and to pay the hefty attorney fees, those handling probates must often sell the deceased's real estate. Thus, we have the "probate sale." The person handling the sale is either the administrator or the executor. (An "administrator" is a court-appointed fiduciary; an "executor" is a fiduciary nominated in a will and approved by the court.)

Selling Property in Probate

An administrator is frequently an attorney. An executor may be either an attorney or a layperson. In either case it frequently becomes their responsibility to dispose of real estate. For example, we'll say that Joseph died several months ago. Since he didn't leave a will (died intestate), an administrator has been appointed by the court to handle the probate.

Joe left behind a four-bedroom, two-bathroom house. The house has been sitting vacant and the estate has been paying the mortgage on it. Since the estate needs money (to pay creditors and attorney fees), the administrator has decided to sell the house.

The administrator has several options here. She can list the house with a real estate agent. She can try to sell it herself on the open market, sort of "by owner" (the estate theoretically owns the house, but the administrator runs the estate). Or she can simply call up an investor friend of hers and ask him if he might want to buy it. The administrator in theory can even buy the property herself, but that is unlikely because it could be construed as a conflict of interest. (The administrator or executor is responsible for getting the best deal for the estate.)

Regardless of what course the administrator or executor selects, the sale *must be approved by the court.* Let's follow through to see how this works.

Following Through on a Probate Sale

We'll say that the administrator or executor decides to go as public as possible and lists the property with a real estate agent; thus the property will probably appear on the multiple-listing service of the local real estate board. The house will probably have a sign posted, and it may even be advertised; in addition there will be a listed price.

I recently observed a probate sale handled in this fashion not far from where I live. The houses in the area had a market value of $150,000.

The probate house was listed for $115,000. Needless to say, it caused quite a stir.

Probate property must be appraised; the price usually can be no less than 90 percent of appraisal. But such appraisals are often notoriously low. Soon there were 11 offers on the property!

The executor received all the offers *but could not accept any of them*. In a probate sale, only the court can accept an offer. The executor set a date on which *all* the offers were to be presented to the court.

At the appointed time and place at the county courthouse, the judge brought up the matter of the probate sale. The executor dutifully presented all 11 offers. They ranged from a low of $105,000 to a high of $118,000. (Several people had bid more than the asking price!)

The judge examined the offers to be sure they were legitimate (filled out sales offer, with an appropriate deposit in the form of a cashier's check) and then took the highest bid, saying, "I'm opening the bidding at $118,000. Will anyone bid higher?"

All of the people who had made offers (or their representatives) could now raise their bids. In addition, *anyone* at all who came into the courtroom and could establish credentials as a legitimate bidder (by having 5 percent of the bid price in a cashier's check) could also bid.

The bidding started and moved up by thousands of dollars, then by hundreds, and then by fifties. The highest *final* bid was $129,850. The judge sold the house to that person, an individual who hadn't even bothered earlier to submit an offer to the executor!

Note two important things. First, making a written offer to an executor or administrator may not amount to a hill of beans in a probate sale. It is showing up at the sale and bidding that takes priority. Second, even though there was strong competition in this case, the final price was still a bargain, probably more than $20,000 below market value.

Finding Out about Probate Sales

In our example the administrator took the most public means of letting people know about the sale. Finding out about probates like these are easy. Just contact any broker.

Unfortunately, sales such as this tend to be the exception. More often than not I have seen executors and administrators "vest-pocket" the sale, which means that they pretty much kept it to themselves. Of course, they can't keep the sale entirely quiet, since the court could accuse them of impropriety or conflict of interest and dismiss them. But in most cases the administrator or executor will do only the minimum necessary. This usually means advertising the property to be sold in a legal paper. The ad need not be enticing, of course, nor might the paper it is published in have a wide circulation. Nevertheless, it's enough for the watchful bargain hunter.

If you watch a legal newspaper closely, you should see advertisements for probate sales crop up. Even if you don't see advertisements for real estate sales themselves, notices of probate most certainly will appear (giving creditors notice that they only have a limited time in which to make their claims). Since there frequently is real estate to be sold, simply calling the administrator or executor *anytime* you see a probate notice should result in a fair number of opportunities to bid on properties.

Remember, regardless of how close to the vest an administrator wants to handle the disposal of real property, at some point advertising will occur. And even if the administrator won't accept an offer from you, you can always show up at the sale and make your bid along with everyone else.

Financing and the Probate Sale

Death does not wipe out a mortgage. Thus, if I own mortgaged property and die and that property is sold through probate, the mortgage continues in force. If you buy that property, you therefore buy it subject to the mortgage.

This is an important concept. You may be bidding on a property at the $100,000 level, but there may be a $70,000 mortgage on it. Thus, the most the estate can hope to receive is $30,000.

By finding out about the probate property well in advance, you can contact the lender and see if you can assume the mortgage. If you can, then you only need to come up with $30,000 instead of $100,000.

If you don't have sufficient cash to assume the mortgage, then perhaps you can make arrangements with a bank, savings and loan, or mortgage banker to prefinance your purchase. You'll have to qualify as to credit. And you'll probably want to get an appraiser out to qualify the property. Once you have done these two things, a lender should be willing to give you a firm loan commitment; for example, 80 percent of your purchase price up to a maximum amount. Now when you bid, you need come up with substantially less.

Alternatively, the estate can sometimes agree to handle the financing itself. Perhaps instead of cash, the estate wants a long-term mortgage that it can give to the heirs. Perhaps the estate is willing to offer 90 percent financing to you, if you have proper credit.

Of course you would need to negotiate with the administrator about this. And you'd be unlikely to get court approval for such favorable terms unless the price you paid was closer to market value. Nevertheless, in this fashion you could arrange financing whereby you only needed to put up 10 percent. (To see how to raise the 10, 20, or 30 percent down without using your own money, see Chapter 14.)

Getting Started

Get a copy of your local legal paper. Look for advertisements for services that cover probates; sometimes there are services which, for a fee, will provide you with detailed information well in advance on probate sales. If there are no services, check the paper for probates and probate sales. Also, check with your real estate broker for any listed probate properties.

Investigate. Call the executor or administrator. This is just a person like you or me, one who will probably (though not always) be delighted to receive your call. Get as much information as you can. Look at the property. Evaluate it. Go to your S&L or bank and arrange for the financing. Show up on auction day. Bid! You, too, can purchase probate property.

Pitfalls

There are tricks to auctions. You will want to be sure you know all the loans there are on the property. Check the title on the property first. Insist on a title report and title insurance from the selling estate as a condition of your purchase.

Check the property's condition and occupancy. Sometimes these properties stand neglected for months and can have considerable damage. In other cases they are rented out. Sometimes relatives are living in them. Be sure you know that you can get any residents out.

Take a dry run first. Probate sales are complex financial purchases. The first time, do everything as if you were going to bid and purchase— but instead of opening your mouth, just stand and watch. You could learn an enormous amount.

Tax Sales

There are two kinds of tax sales that we'll cover: Internal Revenue Service (IRS) tax sales and State tax sales. Both involve taking a property away from its owner by force and selling it "on the courthouse steps" to the highest bidder in order to raise money to satisfy a tax debt.

IRS Tax Sales

You can pick up a lot of good deals here (sometimes incredible bargains), but you must be extraordinarily careful and you must be prepared to risk a lot. IRS tax sales are usually "as is" and "without warranty," meaning that you are on your own.

The IRS is the only branch of government that can seize property and sell it without due process of law. That's an important concept, and few people realize it. When the IRS acts, it can move swiftly and the taxpayer may have few legal recourses—regardless of who is in the right or wrong!

Andrea was a freelance artist who made good money working for advertising agencies. While her artistic skills were excellent, her accounting abilities left a great deal to be desired. Andrea simply never got around to filing her income taxes, ever.

She owned a marvelous brown Porsche and a nice three-bedroom, two-bathroom house in a good section of town. She worked hard, so hard that she paid little attention to the letters and phone calls she had been getting from the IRS. (Yes, there are indeed people like Andrea, in case you're wondering.) One day, as she came out of her house, she found her Porsche gone. As she turned around a federal agent plastered a sticker on her door. It announced that her house had been seized. The agent said her car had also been seized.

Andrea now had 2 weeks to come up with back taxes for 7 years, which the IRS calculated at close to $53,000, including interest. Unless that money was paid *in cash,* her house and car would be auctioned off.

Needless to say, Andrea was in a state of panic. She didn't have any savings and she couldn't raise the money from friends. So her property went to auction.

The IRS auction IRS auctions are held fairly regularly out of main offices of the tax collection service. Times and places are posted, and an application to bid is available.

When you show up to bid, you must usually pay for the item either in cash or with a cashier's check. For some large items a deposit may be accepted with final payment due a few days later.

The IRS auction is final, and you'll get a bill of sale from the IRS. That's pretty good evidence of title for personal property. Still, there could be problems. With a car, a lien held by a lender might still be valid. With a house, it could be that mortgages are still in force after the IRS sale. (It's a bit tricky. The IRS lien comes first, allowing the property to be sold, but the mortgages may continue in force beyond the sale.)

For this reason the IRS seems to avoid seizing heavily mortgaged property, instead preferring real estate that is free and clear. Nevertheless, as a buyer you probably won't have any guarantees as to the nature of the title. It's up to you to find out for yourself. In addition, you probably won't get any title insurance. And if you buy and then try to resell, you may have trouble getting a title company to insure the title with only your tax receipt from the sale.

With all these problems, is it any wonder that bargains are available? Sometimes you can get property for 25 percent of its market value at these sales.

For the person who has cash to spare and doesn't mind taking the risk, looking into IRS tax sales might be a good idea. Don't expect a rose garden, and do be prepared to get speared on a few thorns, but with luck you could become a big winner.

Call the IRS regional center nearest you and ask for information on IRS tax sales. They will direct you to the nearest office.

Property Tax Sales

Each county and state collects property taxes. (Actually, the counties collect the taxes, but much of the money is then forwarded to the state for distribution.) The property taxes become a lien on real estate and are due at a certain date each year. (In California, for example, the first installment is due on December 10, and the second on April 10.) If the taxes are not paid by a deadline date, then the property is sold to the state.

Unlike the IRS, however, the state usually allows a long period of redemption (5 years in California and in many other states). During that time the owner can redeem the property by paying the back taxes and penalties.

Property taxes are a priority lien; they come before any mortgages. This means that once the property is sold to the state, any mortgages on it are normally wiped out. Virtually all mortgages (and trust deeds) therefore contain clauses which allow the lender to pay the delinquent taxes, add the money thus spent to the mortgage, and foreclose. This is for the lender's protection.

Thus, most properties that get sold to the state for back taxes and are not subsequently redeemed are free and clear (that is, the mortgage lender did not pay the taxes to bail out the property). These properties are usually improved lots and older, smaller homes.

Those properties taken back by the counties are usually sold to the public once or twice a year at tax lien sales. The property goes to the highest bidder. Lots valued at a $1000 might sometimes sell for $100, and homes for a quarter of their value. Because the state really doesn't care about getting market price and because few people know about and attend these sales, there are some real bargains available.

The successful bidder gets a "tax deed," which is normally sufficient to get title insurance.

How to take advantage of property tax sales   To find out about tax sales, you must contact the appropriate person in each county or township. That could be the county assessor, tax collector, recorder, or other person whose duties are to handle the sale. This person will provide you with a list of properties and the time of the sale.

As a bidder, it is your responsibility to:

1. Inspect the property and determine its condition. (Properties are usually sold "as is.")
2. Get your own title report and title insurance.
3. Secure your own prefinancing.
4. Determine the property's true value and how much you are willing to pay.

Then it's more or less like the other sales. You show up at the time of the sale, have the stated minimum deposit either in cash or in a cashier's check, and bid on your property.

If you've done your homework, found a good property, made sure of its condition and financing, and bid an appropriate amount, you could just have made the bargain investment of your life!

For more information on property tax sales, check into my book *Wealth Builders* (Franklin Watts, New York, 1985), in which I covered the subject in greater detail.

Consigned Auctions

These are in a kind of middle ground between REOs and forced sales. Here we have properties which have been taken back through foreclosure by a wide variety of participants in the lending field. These include:

Banks

S&Ls

Small Business Administration (SBA)

Federal Deposit Insurance Corporation (FDIC)

Federal Savings and Loan Insurance Corporations (FSLIC)

Other private and government agencies

What all these lenders or insurers have in common is that, in one way or another, through foreclosure they now own real estate that they want to dump.

In Chapters 6 and 7 we talked about how such REOs are normally marketed. However, in some cases the lenders will choose a different approach. They will consign a group of properties to an auction broker, who will then hold a public auction (like those at which rare paintings or coins are sold) and auction the properties to the highest bidder.

These auction houses are located in most big cities. (In Los Angeles, for example, a frequent real estate auctioneer is Kennedy-Wilson of Santa Monica.) To publicize the aution, they may take out full-page ads in leading newspapers. They may also prepare an expensive catalog featuring color photos of the properties involved. Set days are usually given for inspection of the property.

The terms of the sale vary. Some lenders, such as S&Ls, will offer their regular REO terms, such as below-market interest rates and minimum down payments. Others, such as the FDIC and SBA, usually insist on all cash, with no financing.

On some properties there may be a minimum price (called a "reserve" in auction parlance), while on others any bid may be accepted. I recently looked at several such parcels. They were condominiums on which the minimum bid was about $70,000 and the "asking price" was $140,000. (The asking price is just a guide set to try to get buyers thinking about higher prices.)

In researching them, I determined that the comparable market value for these particular units was actually in the $120,000 range. I attended the sale and watched the units go for between $112,000 and $116,000. Not a terrific bargain, but given the preferential financing, not terrible either.

Bidding

To bid in an auction, you normally must get qualified. This means submitting bank and credit references. Once you're qualified, the auction house issues you an ID card, and then you flash that card when you make a bid. If you've ever been to any sort of auction (from antiques to autos), you know what it's all about.

The conditions of the auction are set by the auctioneer, and sales are final and binding. If you bid, you own it and must pay for it.

The auction itself can get pretty heated, with excitement bubbling over in the participants. Sometimes properties go for just the minimum. Other times, on a hot property, the price will go far above market value. Often emotion rather than common sense rules at the auctions.

Your Responsibilities

You've got very little protection in an auction. It's up to you to inspect the property for condition and occupancy, check the title, find out about the financing, and handle all the other work. The auction houses, however, will frequently see to it that the lenders give you a policy of title insurance. In addition, your biggest responsibility is to see to it that there really is a bargain. That is, you've got to determine what the highest price you can afford to pay is—and then bid no higher.

Nowhere in real estate does the real excitement of selling come across more than in the auction. It's fun. And if you're careful and persistent, you can make substantial profits.

The Bottom Line

Forced sales can offer big profits to the bargain hunter. But they're not for everyone. They are for those who are careful, who arrange their financing in advance, who check out the properties, and who are willing to take the risks.

11

Motivated Sellers

"One man's wine is another man's poison," or so goes the old saw. So it can also be in real estate. What can be a horrible property to one person can be a treasure to another.

For one reason or another, some sellers are "motivated" (a term frequently used by brokers in reference to sellers who are willing to make the concessions necessary to sell a property quickly). They want desperately to get rid of a house or office building or lot. To accomplish this, they are willing to lower the price or offer enticing terms, or both. On the other side can be the bargain hunter, for whom a lower price or better terms (or both) is just what he or she is looking for. Put a motivated seller together with the bargain hunter and you can have a marriage made in heaven.

Who Are Motivated Sellers?

Sellers can be motivated for a wide variety of reasons. Some of the reasons may be personal and have nothing to do with the property. Others can be directly related to the real estate itself. Here are just a few of the reasons that a seller may be:

Can't manage the property (can't collect rents)

Payments too high

Just don't like the property

Divorce

Job relocation

Lost job, and now facing foreclosure

Death in family

There are other motivations, of course, but whatever the actual distress may be, it motivates the seller to act quickly. Hence, we find a bargain.

Moral Considerations

It's important here to understand that when we speak of dealing with motivated sellers, we are not talking about taking advantage of someone. The bargain hunter did not create the problem for the seller, and is not contributing to it. Rather, the bargain hunter is offering a solution.

It's easiest to understand this in economic terms. If you're selling something and you aren't motivated, you can ask the highest price and offer the least desirable terms. Because you're not motivated to sell, you can sit back and wait months, or perhaps years, until the market catches up with you and a buyer finally thinks that what you're offering is worthwhile.

On the other hand, if you are highly motivated to sell, you can't afford to wait. You want to deal now, immediately, today. Consequently, you must lower your price and offer more desirable terms. You keep on making the property increasingly attractive until you finally induce a buyer to make a quick purchase.

In terms of who's doing whom a favor, the seller is doing the buyer a favor by offering a more attractive deal—and the buyer is doing the seller a favor by purchasing the property fast. It's a mutually beneficial arrangement that makes sound economic sense.

Finding Motivated Sellers

Motivated sellers can be anywhere. Their property may be listed with brokers. It may be offered for sale by the owner (FSBO). It may not yet even be on the market.

Pete was a bargain hunter. He made no secret of the fact. He had gotten to know half a dozen different brokers in his area, and they were all out scouting property for him (see Chapter 12, "Getting Brokers to Really Work for You").

One day, a broker named Susan called him. She told him of a property she had discovered. It had a motivated seller. Pete listened carefully.

The property was a house in an average area of the city. It had just been listed by another broker, who had put it on the multiple-listing service. It would be a day or two before a *written* notice of the listing went out to all the brokers who belonged. But information on the property was immediately available to any agent who wanted it through the computerized listing service. As soon as a property was listed, it came on the system.

Susan made it a point to check her computer each morning and found the property there. She had promptly investigated it.

Offering a Bargain for a Quick Sale

The owner wanted a quick sale, that week if possible, and as short an escrow as could be arranged. He had lung cancer, knew he was dying, and just wanted to dump the house and move across the country to spend the rest of his days where he grew up. His motivation was that he knew he didn't have a lot of time. He wanted to sell within one or two days.

His house was a three-bedroom, two-bathroom model. In his area, this model normally sold for $105,000 in good condition. His property was in good condition. Moreover, he had added on a new fourth bedroom and a dining room. In addition, he had converted the garage to a family room and built a separate detached two-car garage. Finally, he had poured a lot of concrete so that there was room to park a recreational vehicle by the side of the house.

The additions added a minimum of $10,000 to the value of the property, making it at least a $115,000 house. However, to be sure of a quick sale, he was asking what he felt he had in the property—$89,950. The house was at least $25,000 below market.

Susan suggested that Pete immediately look at the property and make an offer. Pete took his lunch hour to examine the property and then made an offer. He offered full price.

Susan presented the offer at three o'clock that afternoon. The seller accepted, provided that Pete would release $2500 from escrow to him as soon as he signed off; the seller wanted to be able to leave at once.

Normally, releasing money from escrow is a bad practice; if the deal doesn't close, you could lose your money. However, Pete agreed—provided that a preliminary title report showed the property had no title defects and provided that the seller signed off all documents. Three days later Pete released the money and the seller left. Three weeks later the property transfer was formalized.

Pete had used an agent to find a highly motivated buyer to make a quick profit. While motivated sellers such as this don't crop up every day, they are out there. (You will see in Chapter 12 how to get agents to find them for you.)

Desperately Seeking a Way Out

June was a bargain hunter looking for motivated owners. Her specialty was apartment buildings. She would drive around the city looking at such buildings. When she found one that looked run-down, she would contact a tenant to find out who the owner was, then call up the owner and ask if he or she would like to sell.

Most owners said that they would indeed like to sell. But they immediately asked a price that was unreasonably high, usually higher than the market value of their property. They weren't motivated to sell, hence, they could ask any price and then sit back and wait.

Eventually June inquired about an eight-unit building in a less desirable part of the city. She had thought this might be a winner for her because three of the units were vacant, the place was dilapidated (nothing serious, just needed some TLC), and the tenant she spoke to laughed at the mention of the landlord saying that she was 3 months behind in her rent.

The Absentee Landlord

The property owner was a draftsman who worked in a neighboring city. He had traded two rental houses he owned for the apartment building, which had been nothing but a headache ever since. At first he had used a management company to handle the building's rentals. However, the management fee was a thorn in his side. When fully rented, the building brought in $2400 per month, which just equaled the payments. However, the management fee was 15 percent more, or another $360 that he had to take out of his pocket each month. In disgust, he had finally fired the management company.

That's when his troubles really started. He didn't have the time or the mental fortitude to go around collecting rents. So he let things slide. Now most of the tenants were months behind. His half-hearted attempts at renting had not worked. He just didn't have time to run out and show the property when a prospective tenant wanted to see it. He had gone from the frying pan into the fire, for in place of paying just a management fee, he was now taking even more money out of his pocket to cover the mortgage payments.

The owner had a headache and desperately wanted to get rid of it. He had a $50,000 equity in the property from the two rental houses he'd traded for it. He said he wanted to save his equity, or as much of it as possible, but he also wanted to get rid of the property in the worst way. It had been interfering with his work. He was sorry he had ever heard about it. He was thinking of listing it that week with a broker.

June told him not to list, or else she would not buy. She also said she'd be back with an offer in 24 hours.

June did some homework. The property was worth $200,000 and it had $150,000 in loans against it. The owner wanted out in the worst way.

June's Offer

June offered the owner $165,000. She would assume the existing financing and give him a note for $15,000. She would put out no cash of her own.

The owner was at first flabbergasted, then angry. "You're trying to steal my property!" he exclaimed.

"Not at all," she said. "If you try to sell it, you'll have to knock down the price by at least $10,000 because of the way it shows. It's got vacancies, the tenants you have aren't all paying, and it looks like a mess. I'll have to take money out of my pocket to fix up the place.

"In addition, you'd have to pay a commission if you sold it through an agent. Assuming the commission was 6 percent, that's another $12,000. If you add those two amounts together, it comes to $22,000. That's your basic deduction for selling the property, and it lowers your net proceeds from the sale to $178,000.

"Then you'd have to sit on the property for 6 months or longer waiting for it to sell. During that time you'd be losing thousands by making up mortgage payments, taxes, and insurance out of your own pocket. I'm offering you $165,000 to make a deal today. Take my price and you'll be done with your headache immediately."

Market value in top shape	$200,000
Deductions	
Off for present condition	10,000
Normal 6 percent commission	12,000
Premium for a quick sale	13,000
Total	$ 35,000
June's offer	$165,000

The owner considered only a short time, then took it. June got the property for $35,000 off market value. Of course, she had to do some cleanup work. However, she was an expert at managing; she had the building filled with paying tenants within a month.

Motivated Sellers Are Out There

Both of the above stories are based on true incidents. They are not unusual. Motivated sellers are out there. It may take some creative effort to find them (either by having the help of brokers or looking yourself), but once you do find them you can be on the trail of a real bargain.

There are at least two sources that can lead you to motivated buyers. In the case of investment property, as we saw in the example with June, the biggest headache is management. Some people, a great many people, simply can't handle management. They don't want the stress of collecting rent, of dealing with tenants. Yet because they've heard of all the wonderful profits available in real estate, they've bought investment property. Now they have a bigger financial headache than they ever thought possible. Usually they are taking money out of their pockets each month just to keep the property solvent. They think of their investment as a running wound, one that they would do almost anything to get rid of.

For the bargain hunter, therefore, one source is to search for badly managed property. This can be anything from a single family residence to an office building. Badly managed property stands out. It looks bad. Once you find one, locate the owner. It doesn't hurt to ask if he or she wants to sell, and it could result in a great bargain.

Another source is the seller with a personal problem. As in our first example, the seller may want to sell quickly because of personal necessity. This seller is just hoping that a buyer will come along to take the property off his or her hands. Again, enter the bargain hunter who has alerted brokers and others that he or she can offer financial solutions to people with personal difficulties.

Pitfalls When Dealing With Motivated Sellers

The new bargain hunter must be aware, however, that dealing with motivated sellers is not all a bed of roses. It's often much more complex than the two examples we have shown. Typically there are three major problem areas.

The Unsolvable Management Problem

In our second example, June was quickly able to solve the property's problem through disciplined management. (For help here, see the *Hand-*

book of Property Management, Robert Irwin (ed.), McGraw-Hill, New York, 1985.) However, some properties have problems that are too big to solve. These include cases where the property is in a slum and social conditions make good management impossible; where the property is in violation of some city building and safety code and would cost a small fortune to correct; where there is a tenant association that is uncooperative and makes effective management impossible; or where some other uncorrectable problem exists.

The Unsolvable Personal Problem

Sometimes the seller has a problem which can't be solved by a quick sale. In the first example, our owner might instead have desperately needed money for treatment of his illness. He might have wanted to sell his house to raise money, yet still may have wanted to stay there. In this situation the proper answer for him might have been to refinance, not sell. With a refinance the owner could get money out, yet keep the property. A knowledgeable bargain hunter should see this and point it out to the would-be seller.

Note: It's important not to take unfair advantage of sellers motivated by financial need. There's a moral imperative here. In addition, there's a legal one, for an overzealous bargain hunter who takes unfair advantage of a seller's personal condition (particularly when it involves illness, either mental or physical) could be liable for a lawsuit, recision of the transaction, and penalties. The idea is to provide a real solution to a seller's problem, not to browbeat an unwilling and weak seller into accepting an undesirable offer.

The Unsalable Property

Be sure that the seller's property is salable. Some properties are over-mortgaged. Sure, the seller desperately wants out, but that seller may have no equity or even a negative equity. There may be no solution that you can offer here.

The Bottom Line

Highly motivated sellers frequently offer bargain opportunities. Those bargain hunters who can take advantage of the opportunity are investors who can offer solutions and provide a mutually beneficial transaction.

12

Getting Brokers to Work for You

A lament that I've heard over and again is: "A broker won't find a bargain for me. If the broker stumbled across a bargain property, why he'd would surely buy it for himself!" Makes sense, right?

Wrong! If you think the above statement makes sense, then you really don't understand most agents. In this chapter we're going to examine what motivates agents and how to get them to help you.

Why You Need the Help of Real Estate Brokers

As a bargain hunter, you need all the help you can get to find good properties. That goes without saying. But above all, you need the aid of real estate agents. Agents work full-time at locating properties. There are few bargain hunters who can get to know the market as well as agents do. The truth is that in most cases agents are the ones who stumble across and then list most of the real bargains.

I have read books by those who advocate bypassing the agent. "Go directly to the source," some advocate, "—go to the seller. That way you can save the commission." It sounds good. But how many of us have the time, the fortitude, and the endurance to spend the better part of every day scouting real estate?

Agents offer a nationwide system already established for marketing real estate. Everyone in this country knows about brokers. Nearly everyone uses them at one time or another. To my way of thinking, trying to create your own system of locating property when such an efficient and widespread system is already in existence doesn't make sense.

Don't try to circumvent the broker. Get the broker to do your work for you. Put the established real estate marketing system to work for you. It won't cost you money. As we'll see, it will make you more money in the long run.

Understanding Real Estate Agents

Some bargain hunters see the broker as an adversary, or at best as a competitor. That's the wrong way to look at it. Yes, of course the agent can be a competitor, but only if you make that agent one. You can just as easily appeal to another part of the agent that will motivate that person to be on your side, to want to help you.

The motivating principle is the commission. Real estate agents make their living on commissions. Offer an agent a commission and that agent will do just about anything for you, including in most cases helping you buy the bargain property that he or she was thinking of buying. Here's why.

The Real Estate Agency Business

Contrary to popular belief, real estate is a hard business and not particularly well-paying. The statistics I've seen indicate that most agents make under $25,000 a year. A great many make under $15,000. Very very few make over $75,000. Although they may be dealing in properties worth hundreds of thousands of dollars, they themselves don't make much money.

For many of us that seems hard to believe. After all, if an agent gets a 6 percent commission, for example, and sells a $100,000 property, there's $6000 right there. It doesn't take many of those sales to add up to big income, does it?

Yes, it does!

Most sales are "cobrokered," which means that there are two real estate companies involved, one bringing in the seller and the other the buyer. In such cases the commission is often split in half. In addition, within a company a salesperson may have made the deal. That means a further split between the buyer's and the seller's agent. That big fat $6000 commission can suddenly turn into a piddling $1500 commission to each of four individuals.

If a top salesperson makes one sale a month (which is considered pretty good in the business) and only makes $1500 per sale, that comes to only $18,000 a year. Hardly a royal salary. (Remember, out of that income the agent must also pay for heavy car usage and sometimes for advertising and phone expenses.)

Hungry for Business

As a result, most real estate agents are always hard-pressed for cash. Of course, the agents would indeed love to invest in real estate themselves. Their more urgent concern, however, is making commissions in order to survive.

Now, enter the bargain hunter who's looking for some good opportunities in real estate. You've talked to the real estate agent, explaining just what you're looking for (I'll talk about how to get an agent to remember you in a few paragraphs), and one day the agent comes across a good piece of property. Will the agent buy it or call you?

My experience has been that the agent will almost always call you first! The thought of a cash commission almost always outweighs other considerations in the mind of the agent. Getting that commission is the goal. Remember, most agents are in the real estate business first, and the investment business second.

Agents Who Invest

That's not to say that agents don't invest in real estate. They do, and as often as possible. But typically they buy a property only when they find that they have no opportunity to sell it to someone else. A bargain property appears and the agent tries to find a bargain hunter, but can't. Now the agent is faced with losing out entirely (having another agent make the sale) or personally buying the property. In this case the agent will try to buy.

The problem, however, is that it isn't easy for an agent to invest. Agents need cash like everyone else. In addition, lenders are always suspicious of agents who are buying property and usually require stiffer qualifications for financing.

The Agent Will Work for You

As a result, and contrary to common belief, a real estate broker will work hard for a bargain hunter and will show you prime properties as they appear. This isn't theory. Other bargain hunters and I have seen it work in practice time and time again. Brokers will work hard to find you bargains. After all, their business is selling real estate to collect commissions. Yours is finding bargain properties and making a profit. The two businesses make a very nice blend.

The key, however, is to convince the brokers that you can indeed make them a commission. If you're the sort who hesitates in the face of an obvious bargain, if you don't have any money (or appear not to), or if it in any way appears as though you're going to cheat the brokers out of their commissions, forget it—because they'll forget you.

How to Get a Loyal Agent

Brokers thrive on loyalty. They long for loyal buyers. Selling real estate is a highly competitive business, and brokers realize that there is nothing to prevent you from working for months with one person and then, after that person has found just the property you are looking for, buying through someone else. Any broker who's been in the business any length of time knows the problems of disloyalty intimately.

Therefore, when you first approach a real estate agent, the foremost question in that agent's mind is going to be "If I work hard and find the right bargain, will this person buy from me?" I know an agent whose first question when dealing with an investor is: "What's my competition? How many other agents are you going to be asking to find bargains?" The amount of effort she puts into the bargain hunter's search is directly commensurate with the number of other agents involved. If she's the only agent, she works hard. If she's one of a dozen, she doesn't work at all. Oh, if something turns up, she'll call, after she's called all the other bargain hunters who are working closely with her.

Therefore, any way that you can convince the agent that you really are working only with him or her alone will be to your advantage.

The Exclusive Buyer's Agreement

If you've already bought or sold property through a broker, then you've established a bond, and getting that broker to work for you in the future shouldn't be a problem. On the other hand, if you're new to it, it could be difficult. I suggest the following:

1. Map out a specific area: a neighborhood, a small town, or any other well-defined region.

2. Visit a dozen or so brokers in the area and determine which is the most active and the most knowledgeable. (You'll be able to tell this after awhile just by talking a few minutes with an agent. Many simply won't know the territory. Others will know it intimately.)

3. Once you find a broker whose knowledge and abilities you trust, give that broker an exclusive buyer's agreement *for the specified area for a specified period of time.*

An exclusive buyer's agreement states that if you buy property within a specific area, you agree to buy it only through the named broker. It's like a listing—only instead of listing property, you're listing your intention to purchase. The agreement doesn't prevent you from buying property through another agent; it just means that you'd have to pay a commission to the broker with whom you listed if you bought elsewhere.

Once you've given the agent the exclusive buyer's agreement, that agent should feel a certain loyalty from you . . . and for you. After all, you've committed yourself to buy through that agent.

Limiting the Agreement

It's important to understand, however, that real estate is a localized business. An agent who, for example, knows the south side of town like the palm of his hand may not know much about the east side.

Similarly, we all are prone to making errors. We might think that an agent is just perfect for us, only to discover a month later that he's a turkey who never works.

Consequently, it is important to put at least two limitations on the buyer's agreement. The first limits the territory: The agreement only applies *if* you buy property within certain specific boundaries—the agent's home field. The second limit the time: If the agent hasn't found a property for you within, say, 30 days, then the agreement ends and you'll try another agent.

How to Keep Agents Loyal

Finally, having once found good agents, it's important to keep them loyal. You do this by paying them and not cheating them out of a commission.

The temptation here can be great. Sheila was the sort of bargain hunter who not only wanted a bargain but also wanted to be sure that she was the only one who profited from it.

Sheila signed a buyer's agreement with Chuck, an agent. Within 3 weeks Chuck produced a property. It had a market value of $150,000, but Chuck could get it for Sheila for $120,000. She dove for it and the deal was made.

Worrying About the Commission

However, Sheila began thinking about that commission. Since Chuck had both listed and sold the property, he was getting a full commission, in this case 7 percent, or $8400. She spoke to Chuck, saying, "This was too easy. You didn't have to work for the commission. You just called me up and I bought the property. You should give me at least half."

Chuck was appalled. He thought of all those weeks and months he'd spent searching for properties. He remembered the times he'd been beaten out by other agents, been humiliated by buyers or sellers who bought elsewhere, and suffered long, dry periods without sales. Immediately his opinion of Sheila went down a notch. Nope, he said, he wouldn't split his commission.

Sheila saw that he was serious, so she considered. She was putting $10,000 down on the property. Most of that money the seller would give to Chuck as his commission. She had an idea.

Taking Advantage of the Broker

Sheila waited until the deal was ready to close. Then she announced that she'd had a financial turn of events. The money she'd had to make the deal was now committed elsewhere. She couldn't go through with it.

The seller was angered and threatened to sue both Sheila *and* Chuck. Chuck was mortified. What was Sheila thinking?

Then Sheila announced that she would make the sale *if* instead of putting $10,000 down, she only had to put $1500 down. The balance could be in the form of a third mortgage to the seller.

The seller thought it was great. That was just the amount he owed Chuck. If Chuck would take a third mortgage for $8500 for his commission instead of cash, the deal could still go through.

The ball was now in Chuck's court. He could of course refuse. But then he would lose the sale altogether (since other agents were aware of the property and had offers ready to present if the deal fell through). In addition, he might be named in a lawsuit by the seller. On the other hand . . . Chuck accepted. The third mortgage was written—no payments, no interest, and all due and payable in 5 years—and the seller transferred it to Chuck.

As soon as the deal was closed, Sheila approached Chuck. She said she was sorry that things had worked out the way they had, particularly since her finances had now cleared and she had some money. To help straighten things out, she would be willing to buy that third mortgage off Chuck for cash *for half its value.*

Chuck could wait 5 years to collect or take cash now. As anyone who knows the future value of money will tell you, it was no choice at all. Chuck took it.

Sheila was all smiles. She got the property and half the commission. But Chuck was no fool. He knew exactly how he had been played. Not only would he never ever give another bargain opportunity to Sheila, he would also see to it that as many other agents as possible knew about her and stayed away.

Yes, Sheila got her great bargain, but she probably lost out on many more bargains in the future.

The Moral

The moral here is simple—don't bite the hand that feeds you. In a good deal there's more than enough money to go around. Let the agents have their share and they'll come back later with more for you. Try to get more than your share and you can take yourself out of the market.

My Bias

Now that you've read this chapter, I'm sure you're wondering about my own bias. Does the chapter sound as if it's been written by an agent? If so, should what is being said here be taken with a grain of salt?

Yes, I hold a real estate broker's license and have done so for the last 25 years. However, I have not acted as an agent (listing or selling for others) for the last 20 years. In fact, I didn't make any money in real estate until I stopped working as an agent and became an investor for myself. To this day, whenever I buy or sell real estate I always try to use an agent—and I always pay the commission.

13

Hidden Treasures in Financing

There's an old saw about real estate that goes something like this. Two fellows are considering the purchase of a skyscraper in Manhattan. The first one says, "The deal's in the bag. We can buy the building for only a hundred million dollars."

The second one says, "Sounds terrific, let's do it."

The first replies, "There's one snag, though. They want $500 in cash!"

In real estate, financing has always been the key. As we've noted earlier, it may not be the price or the condition or the location of the property that makes the deal—it can be the terms.

In recent years, however, it has become fashionable to think of financing strictly in relationship to leveraging. Bargain terms, or bargain financing, has come to mean buying for little or no down payment (see Chapter 14 for suggestions on getting started on a shoestring), but that's *not* what we're talking about here. In today's market, overleveraging and buying with no down payment can be an invitation to disaster.

Finding a bargain in financing, in fact, rarely means looking for the minimum down payment. Rather, there are other areas that are of strategic importance, such as the specific clauses in the mortgage, its interest rate, and its type.

A Basic Financing Bargain

A friend was recently buying a lakefront lot for investment purposes. The going price for lakefront lots in the area was $110,000. My friend had just closed another deal and that had a fair amount of cash. Since he was looking for a bargain, he offered the owner of one of the lakefronts $80,000 cash for the lot.

That was $30,000 less than the market price. Normally, he wouldn't expect an owner to take such a drastic reduction, but cash usually talks. He had hopes of picking up a price bargain simply by being able to pay for it outright.

The lot owner, however, countered at $105,000. The owner wasn't impressed by cash. (It turned out that she was retired and was befuddled with how she would invest so much cash if she got it.)

My bargain-hunting friend was faced with a dilemma. He had thought to get a price bargain because of his cash offer. Now he discovered that cash wasn't all it was cracked up to be with this owner. So now he did a 180-degree turn and decided to try for a financing bargain. He gave her what she demanded, the full price, $105,000. However, he dictated the terms.

He offered to put 20 percent down. The owner would carry the balance in the form of a mortgage for 15 years at 8 percent interest.

The reason my friend felt this was a bargain was twofold. First, the market interest rate was then 12 percent. (He offered 8 percent.) Second, it's almost impossible to get a mortgage on bare land. If he got the deal, the owner would be financing 80 percent of the purchase price on bare land, a real bargain in itself.

The owner's only quibble was the interest rate. She insisted on 10 percent. But that was still 2 percent below market. And she was willing to give a 15 year loan on a property that no one else would lend money on.

When the price bargain didn't pan out, this bargain hunter sought out and got a financing bargain. (Note that the price was no longer the issue because the terms were so good.)

Understanding Paper

Getting a better than market interest rate or getting a loan which would be otherwise unavailable are two ways to get financing bargains. There are many others. Almost all of these involve the use of "paper."

As those familiar with real estate know, "paper" is a term used to describe a mortgage, typically a mortgage taken back by a seller. When you get a mortgage, you've created paper. If someone says she bought a house for $100,000 with $20,000 down and the seller carried the balance, this means that she came up with $20,000 in cash and that the rest ($80,000) was paper.

Here it's important for us to understand a further division. There is "hard" paper and "soft" paper.

Hard Paper

Sometimes also called a "hard-money mortgage," this is simply an exchange of cash for a mortgage. You want to refinance your home in order to take a cruise to Alaska. You go to a lender who gives you $10,000 in cash, in exchange for which you give the lender a mortgage. Because there was cash advanced, this is "hard paper." A new first mortgage obtained from a lender in order to make a purchase of property would be hard paper.

There is no definitive reason why the term "hard paper" is used except that perhaps this is the hard way to finance.

Soft Paper

Also simply called "paper," this is a mortgage for something other than cash. Almost always it's for equity. A seller wants to get rid of his home. He accepts an offer that calls for him to carry back a second mortgage for $20,000. That amount of money is not advanced in the form of cash to anyone. Rather, it's an equity exchanged for a mortgage. A typical soft-paper transaction might look like this:

Sales price of house	$100,000
Down payment	$10,000
First mortgage assumed by buyer	$70,000
Second mortgage carried by seller (*soft paper*)	$20,000

Note that in the above example the buyer got the benefit of a $20,000 second mortgage without any cash changing hands. Rather, it was the seller who exchanged his equity for the mortgage.

Differences between Hard and Soft Paper

There are two major differences between hard and soft paper. Hard paper almost always carries a much higher interest rate. The reason is that when people advance cash, they want to be sure they are earning an interest rate commensurate with the risk.

Soft paper is more flexible. A seller who is taking back a soft paper second, for example, might just as easily agree to the value of the second being $8000 instead of $10,000 on the purchase of a house. After all, it's the equity that is being exchanged, and it's a lot easier to give up a little equity than to give up cash out of pocket.

Because soft paper is also on equity, not cash, the *interest rate* might be lower, the *terms* longer, and the *conditions* of the loan more favorable. (If we wanted to be precise—as is the case with very large real estate transactions—the exact present value of every mortgage can be calculated from its terms and we could then accurately compare different mortgages. This, however, is a complex process and beyond the scope of this chapter. For our purposes, we need only be concerned with the fact that soft paper is far more flexible than hard.)

All of which is to say that lenders of hard paper (hard money mortgages), such as banks and S&Ls, are less likely to offer bargain terms than are lenders of soft paper, such as sellers.

Using Soft Paper to Get Bargains

Some of the best financing bargains come about through the use of soft paper. Once you as a bargain hunter have determined that what you are going for is a financing bargain (as opposed to a price bargain), then there's almost no limit to the creative kinds of mortgages you can develop. It all comes down to negotiation. In most cases this means giving the seller his or her price and getting the terms to suit you.

Each of the following financing bargains assumes that you as a buyer demand the particular term as a condition of purchase. In other words, if the seller doesn't give you the terms you demand, you won't buy.

Getting a Lower Interest Rate

The most obvious kind of financing bargain is to go for a lower interest rate. A seller carrying back paper and getting full price isn't as likely to quibble about interest rates. Such a seller might be happy to accept 8 percent (when the going rate is 12 percent) just to get the property sold at full price.

In the negotiations the key is to make the condition of sale the interest rate. Yes, you will pay the price, but *only* if the seller accepts the rate you demand.

(*Note:* Accepting a lower-than-market interest rate can be a problem for the seller. Recent tax rulings have indicated that the government may "impute" interest in such cases. This means that sellers might have to pay taxes *as if* they had received market rate, even though they received less!)

Getting a Longer Term

Another bargain area that many hunters overlook is the term. This is particularly the case with bare lots. Most lots are financed by sellers for 3 to 5 years. On the other hand, if you could make a purchase in which the seller agreed to carry the paper for 15 years or longer, it might be a real bargain.

Look at it this way: $30,000 over 3 years at 10 percent interest means that you're going to have to pay $968 a month, or $11,600 a year. On the other hand, $30,000 over 15 years at 10 percent means that you'll pay only $322 a month, or $3864 a year. It could mean the difference between making a profit or taking a loss.

Negative Amortization

Another use of soft paper is to negotiate for lower payments. The seller is carrying back a $50,000 mortgage at 10 percent interest for 15 years. In order to fully amortize (pay off) the mortgage, the payments should be $537 per month.

But you plan on renting out the property and you can't afford to pay more than $450 a month. So you write the mortgage in such a way that your payments only equal $450.

No, that doesn't mean you ultimately pay less. You actually pay more; since you are not paying the full interest due each month, it is added to the mortgage amount (negative amortization), and ultimately you end up owing more than you borrowed. In the meantime, however, you have the advantage of lower payments, which may mean that you can afford to buy a property that you otherwise couldn't afford. (In this case you'd probably figure on refinancing within 5 years to get to a fully amortized, or paid-out, mortgage.)

Deferring the Payments

Yet another financing bargain can be the deferral of payments. You buy a house and the seller carries back a $20,000 second mortgage at 10 percent. You insist that the terms of the mortgage are *no payments at all* until it comes due in 3 years!

For 3 years you can thus have the cash flow from the property (from rental income) without making any payments on the second. In times when prices are rapidly rising, this can be a real bargain. It can allow you to buy property with reduced payments, often meaning no negative cash flow. Of course, at the end of the loan term (3 years in this case) it all comes due, meaning that prices had better have risen so that you can sell or refinance.

Some unscrupulous buyers purchase under these terms and then, if prices don't rise, just walk: They drop the property to foreclosure. A foreclosure against a person's record of course can make it very difficult to get new mortgages in the future. Even if the foreclosure doesn't go against one's record, a reputation as a "walker" will make it difficult for one to deal with buyers in the future.

Paying No Interest

Sometimes sellers are so hung up on price that they are willing to give the buyer interest-free loans. Don't overlook this possibility, rare though it may be. (One of the problems is that the government tends to impute interest, as indicated above. This means that sellers may have to pay taxes on interest they did not receive!)

Getting Special Terms

In addition, bargains can be found in the terms of the mortgage. These include getting a mortgage which offers:

1. No prepayment penalty (so you can pay it off any time)
2. Assumability (so the next buyer can assume it)
3. No penalty for late payments
4. A subordination clause (to be discussed shortly)

Getting Money Back out of the Property

Thus far we've discussed how to get a financing bargain from soft paper at the time you purchase. There's another kind of financing bargain, one that involves getting money out of the property. It is usually done once you have ownership, but in some cases it can be done at the time of purchase.

Simple Refinancing

This is the easiest to understand. You buy a property. It goes up in value. You refinance, getting hard paper (cash for a mortgage), and thus get your money out of your property. Most owners of real estate in the United States in fact did this between 1977 and 1981, when prices were soaring.

Another way of doing this is to buy distressed property and then fix it up, get it reappraised at a higher value, and refinance it. In this way you can get your cash out without having to wait for appreciation.

Yet another way is to buy income property (an apartment building, for example) and increase the rent. Since the property's value depends on the rent amount, an increased rent means that your property has increased in value, and you can thus secure a higher loan and can get your cash out.

Buying Back the Soft Paper

Another method of getting cash out of property involves soft paper. At the time of purchase the bargain hunter gives the seller a mortgage for equity. Then, 6 months later, the bargain hunter says to the seller, "I can cash you out. I'll give you 60 percent of the value of that mortgage in cash to pay it off."

Depending on the terms of the mortgage (particularly if it was written for a long term at a low interest rate), the seller might agree. The bargain hunter now refinances the whole property, getting enough to pay off the existing first *and* the soft-paper mortgage at 60 percent of value. In some cases this can even result in cash going back into the pocket of the buyer!

Cranking the Property

Some bargain hunters specialize in "crankables," a term which means that the financing on the property allows the buyer to "crank" the property for cash—to get cash back out of the property, usually after purchase.

For those new to finance bargain hunting, this may seem a bit complicated, but it really isn't. The best way to understand it is to see how it works.

Tony bought a house for $100,000. He put $10,000 cash down to a $90,000 first mortgage. As soon as the purchase was completed, he went out and got a hard-paper second for $20,000.

In this simple example, Tony's refinance brought him $20,000—enough to pay back the original $10,000 he put down plus put another $10,000 in his pocket. He "cranked" the property for cash.

Tony's Purchase		Tony's Refinance	
Existing first	$ 90,000	Existing first	$ 90,000
Down payment	10,000		
		New second	20,000
Purchase price	$100,000	Total financing	$110,000

Such crankables are easily accomplished in a hot market when property values are rising rapidly, such as last occurred around 1980. In such a market, lenders of hard paper are frequently willing to lend over and above a recent purchase price because of the rapid price appreciation.

In recent years, however, with stagnant appreciation, hard money lenders have been reticent to make such loans. Consequently, in today's market, Tony would have had to buy the property for considerably less than market value in order realistically to be able to crank it as indicated.

The Subordinated Crankable

Another form of the crankable involves a subordinated mortgage. "Subordination" means that a lender agrees to allow a mortgage to remain in a secondary position. We've already touched on this earlier, and I'll explain it in greater detail shortly. First, however, let's see the effect.

For our example we'll take a theoretical case: Jeff bought a six-unit apartment building for $200,000. The financing was simple. He assumed an existing first mortgage for $100,000, and the owner carried back a second mortgage that was subordinated for $100,000.

Now Jeff decided he needed some cash. So he went out and obtained a new first mortgage for $200,000.

Jeff's Old Financing		Jeff's New Financing	
First	$100,000	New first	$200,000
Second	100,000	Second	100,000
Original financing	$200,000	New financing	$300,000

Suddenly where there was $200,000 in financing on the property, there is now $300,000. The difference of $100,000 was in the form of cash, which Jeff put into his pocket. He cranked the property for $100,000.

There are two important points to understand about how this was done. First, Jeff secured a new hard-paper first mortgage. First mortgages for cash are very easy to obtain and the interest rates are highly competitive; when people buy a house, they get a new first. Refinancing as was done here, is almost as easy. (On the other hand, hard-money seconds are much harder to obtain, and the term is usually shorter and the interest rate higher.)

Second, Jeff was able to secure a new hard-money first because the existing second mortgage remained in position. *Because the second contained a subordination clause, it did not advance to first position upon being refinanced.*

Advancement of the secondary mortgage   In Chapter 4 I explained that the order of a mortgage depends on *when it is placed on the property.* The first mortgage was placed first, the second was placed second, and so forth.

As soon as any mortgage is paid off, the mortgages behind it immediately advance in position. This is only logical. If you have a property with three mortgages—a first, a second, and a third—what happens when the first is paid off? You end up with a property that has two mortgages: The second becomes the first and the third becomes the second. The mortgages advance to fill the empty positions—*unless* there is a special clause in the mortgages (a subordination clause) that forces them to remain in their original position.

When Jeff refinanced, he paid off the existing first on the property ($100,000). Normally the second would now advance and become a first; however, the second contained a subordination clause which forced it to remain in position.

Thus, Jeff was able to refinance and get a brand new first while holding the second off. The new first was for twice the amount of the old first. Jeff pocketed that money.

Problems with subordination   What should be apparent is that there is great opportunity for abuse in the subordination clause. If the property was only worth $200,000, then by refinancing the first, Jeff effectively reduced the seller's protection in the property to zero.

Remember, originally the seller gave $100,000 in a second mortgage and Jeff took over an existing $100,000 first. If the property was worth $200,000, that meant that if the seller had to foreclose, there was enough equity to protect his position. On the other hand, after Jeff refinanced, the first was bloated to $200,000—the full value of the property—and the seller's $100,000 second had no protection. It became worthless. (But if the property had had a value of $300,000, then presumably there would have been nothing wrong with refinancing the first for $200,000, since the $100,000 second would still be protected.)

Some sellers have granted subordination clauses in the past (particularly to developers of raw land) only to find that once the new big first was obtained, their interest was unprotected. In the event of foreclosure, they lost everything.

In recent years, sellers who have fallen into this predicament have on occasion sued buyers for fraud. This is a strong reason to avoid abuse of the subordination clause.

Conclusion

Financing bargains abound. They can be in the form of reduced interest rate, increased term, smaller or no payments, or getting cash out of the property. When the price becomes nonnegotiable (or anytime for that matter!), look for a financing bargain.

14

Getting Started on a Shoestring

Do you need a lot of cash to be a real estate bargain hunter?

No, you don't, but it helps. As seen in other chapters, opportunities do exist for those with little or no cash. If, however, you do have some capital, it's a big advantage.

This chapter is for those of us who are getting started here and now and don't have very much cash. You want to become a bargain hunter, but you need some capital to get started. How do you raise it? This chapter gives some clues.

A special word of warning to readers. *Don't* gamble with money you can't afford to lose. If your savings or other cash holdings are irreplaceable and you're counting on them for retirement, health security, or other similar reasons, don't risk them on a real estate bargain. There are no sure things in life and in real estate. You could lose. If you can't afford to lose the money you have, you're probably not the right person to be involved in hunting for bargains. Not everyone is. Only if you have the financial stability to sustain a possible loss and continue on without difficulty should you dabble in investment real estate.

Now, how do you raise the necessary capital? Here are some clues.

Don't Overlook Any Possibilities

How you raise capital to get started in bargain hunting can run the gamut from something simple like cashing in savings bonds to something unusual like putting together a syndicate of your relatives and friends. The important thing to remember is that once you've found a bargain property, you don't want to lose it for lack of capital. When you see the opportunity to make thousands of dollars in quick profits, you don't want to be a dollar short of getting in.

Thus, ideas that may sound outlandish right now while sitting comfortably and reading this book may prove to be lifesavers later on when you desperately need to raise the dollars to buy the property. My suggestion is that you dismiss no notions out of hand.

Someday you may fall into a terrific bargain opportunity and need only a few more dollars in cash to swing it. You're ready to sell your brother's last pair of pants to get the money. When that time comes, remember this chapter. Come back and reread it. Maybe, just maybe one of those ideas that before seemed so unlikely may seem just a bit more practical . . . and possible.

Raising Money for the Down Payment

When I talk about raising capital, what I'm speaking about is raising enough money for the down payment. In almost all cases a large part of the purchase price can be financed. Typically this down payment will be anywhere between 5 and 20 percent of the total cost. That's the amount you'll need to raise in cash. (The balance will come from a mortgage, either from an institutional lender like a bank or from the seller; see Chapter 13.)

The question here is how do you get that down payment?

Note: There are lots of books written on how to buy property *without* a down payment; if you follow their advice, you probably can purchase that way. But here we're concerned with getting *bargains*. In a market where prices aren't appreciating rapidly, getting bargains usually requires some cash. Unless you plan to make hundreds of offers in hopes of finding that one seller who will go along with a no-down scheme and still give you a bargain (a tiring and discouraging plan), it's best to figure you'll need some cash down.

How to Get Cash

You have a variety of ways to raise cash. As I mentioned at the outset, don't discard any of these. You never know when one or another of these ways may pull out just the money you need to make a deal.

Write Check

Too simple? Not if you don't have money in the bank. But planning ahead can help even when you don't have the money. Most banks today allow "reserve" and "overdraft" privileges for customers who first establish a line of credit. Typically, these credit lines allow the customer to write a check to anyone for amounts up to $25,000 without a cash balance. The bank honors the check and converts the money into a short-term loan.

If you're planning to be a bargain hunter, then go down to your bank right now, today, and take out a line of credit on your checking account. Go for the highest limit you can get. It's easiest to establish this credit line *before* you need the money. (Remember, you must pay this money back, so be sure your plan takes this into account.)

Withdraw Your Savings

Strange as it may seem, some bargain hunters plan on doing their investing without touching their savings. Admittedly, bargain hunting is a risky business. But you have to pay the toll to play the game. That may mean depleting your savings account.

(Caution: Don't gamble with money you can't afford to lose.)

Cash In Your Stocks, Bonds, Coin Collection, or Other Investments

Most of us try to diversify our investments. But what if a fantastic real estate opportunity appears? Should we turn it down simply on the general principle of diversification? Maybe. On the other hand, if you're really convinced that this is the deal of the century, perhaps you'll want to consider selling off stocks, bonds, rare coins, diamonds, gold, or whatever other investments you have. If the opportunity truly is good, then maybe you could make more by putting all your eggs in this one basket.

Sell or Refinance Your Property

Do you have any property you can sell? Do you have an investment piece of real estate? What about a boat, car, motorcycle, or even furniture? It's a matter of compromise. Are you desperate enough to sell or refinance some item you now own in order to get the real estate bargain you've found?

Sell Your House (and Move to an Apartment)

I said some of these suggestions would sound outrageous. But consider, you've found a terrific bargain. It can make you thousands, perhaps tens of thousands. You need cash right away, and the only collateral you have is your house. Assuming you can't borrow on it (which we'll consider in a moment), consider selling it. It's an asset, and if you're really desperate, it can get you cash.

Borrow

Finally, if all else fails, you can borrow the money. We've already talked about one form of borrowing—writing a check on a line of credit. In addition, you have many other opportunities for borrowing.

Borrow from an S&L

Savings and loan associations usually won't make unsecured loans. Usually they also won't make loans on other than real estate. They will, however, make all kinds of real estate loans. Can you borrow a hard-paper or hard-money second on the property you're buying or on some other property (such as your home)?

In most cases S&Ls want a first-mortgage position. But some S&Ls for very little more interest will make second mortgages. Some will make thirds (see Chapter 13). Don't overlook these secondary positions for raising cash.

Borrow from a Bank

Banks will make the same kinds of loans that S&Ls will, although they often charge a slightly higher interest rate. In addition, banks will also make loans on other collateral, such as your car, furniture, or stocks. In some cases if you have good credit they will make unsecured loans, that is, a loan on just your good name. If you have good credit, a bank is a "must see" source for cash.

Borrow from a Credit Union

If you belong to a credit union, you can frequently get either a secured or an unsecured loan, often at a favorable interest rate. Don't overlook this possibility. A simple call to your credit union should let you know your chances of getting money from this source.

Borrow on Your Credit Cards

If you have reasonably good credit, you should be able to get a VISA card or MasterCard. If you can get one such card, you can get dozens. Banks and other institutions compete with one another to offer you such cards. For an annual fee of around $25 a card, there probably isn't any limit to the number you can get. (I once knew an individual who had acquired over 200 such cards. I've heard of people who have acquired thousands!) Each card usually offers anywhere from $300 to $5000 in credit. For a short-term loan, you can borrow the limit on each and get a substantial amount of money.

But remember, you'll have to pay it back! Be sure your plan calls for a way to repay the funds with any interest. (Some cards will give you interest-free loans if you repay by the next billing period.)

Borrow from Friends

It's hard to ask friends for loans. On the other hand, if it's the only way to raise money for a terrific opportunity, why not try it? It sometimes helps assuage any feelings of guilt if you offer to repay with interest. Another consolation can be to take the friends in as partners. We'll discuss this shortly.

Borrow from Relatives

If it was hard to ask friends for loans, think about asking relatives. I consider this close to a last resort approach. Nevertheless, if it's the only way . . .

Borrow from a Commercial Finance Company

I do consider this a last resort. Some of these companies will lend you money at very high interest rates only if they tie up virtually all your assets, including both personal and real estate. And they may not feel any restraint at foreclosing, repossessing, and garnishing wages to collect their due.

Use them only if you must. Even then, borrow as little as possible.

Clues on Borrowing

There are lots of books and magazine articles constantly appearing which give you hints on borrowing, including methods of improving your credit. Check with them. In the meantime, here are five clues to borrowing which you may find helpful.

Only Borrow When You Don't Need the Money

Lenders hate loaning to someone in need. They feel that such a person may be desperate enough to exaggerate (if not lie) on loan applications. Therefore, if you really need the money quickly, you may have trouble getting it.

The answer is to arrange for a loan *before* you need it. Get the credit line or loan established. Then, when you find the deal, the money's waiting.

Establish Your Credit

If you have no credit, go into a bank and open a checking account and a savings account. After a month or two, apply for a credit card. Your bank will probably give it to you, although at a low limit. Charge up to the limit and repay promptly.

Now go back to the bank and take out a personal loan. (They'll undoubtedly give this to you based on your checking and savings account and credit card history.) Repay the loan promptly. You should now have credit, enough to get you other credit cards and other loans.

Improve Your Bad Credit

If you can't get a credit card (the one sure sign of bad credit), try buying a house to improve your credit! It's not that hard. Find a seller who will go for nothing or little down (the seller carries a second or third mortgage for the down payment) and who has an existing loan that is fully assumable. (You're not going to get a bargain here. This is just to establish credit.)

Once you get the house, make all the payments promptly. Now reapply for either a bank loan or a credit card. With the house as collateral and with the evidence of prompt payment on the mortgage, you should find it much easier this time around.

Borrow All That You Need the First Time

No lender likes to see the borrower coming back asking for more money. It indicates that the borrower didn't have enough foresight to know how much was needed or miscalculated or is in trouble. You may not get a second chance. Therefore, overestimate your need and borrow the full amount.

Pay Back Promptly

The only thing worse than failure to repay is delayed repayment. A late payment goes on your record every month. (Failure to pay appears only once.) If you value your ability to borrow, *always* repay everything you borrow, promptly.

Sources of Collateral

Lenders want collateral. They want to be able to get at something substantial if you fail to repay what you borrow. (In some cases, if you have very good credit a lender will give you an unsecured loan. If that's your situation, you needn't worry here. Also, you can sometimes get unsecured loans from friends and relatives.) Here are some ideas on what you can put up as collateral:

1. Your house.
2. Other real estate, including lots, second homes, and investment property.
3. Personal property, including car, stereo equipment, and furniture.
4. Your life insurance. If you have a policy which has equitable value, you can probably borrow against it at a bank.
5. Treasury Bills, certificates of deposit, stocks, bonds, second or other mortgages in your favor, or any other financial instrument of value.
6. Your Keogh account (if you're incorporated).
7. Your salary. Sometimes, particularly with banks, just being able to prove ability to repay is sufficient. A steady job means a lot, particularly if it goes with good credit. For more money you might want to try a second job.

Try an Exchange

This is an idea that is too often overlooked. Instead of putting up cash for the down payment, can you get the seller to accept something else?

What about offering a lot you own in trade? What about another piece of investment property? What about a car, motorcycle, boat, furniture, or other item you own? If you have a skill (such as being an accountant or carpenter), can you exchange your future work for the down payment?

You'll never know what the seller will trade for until you ask.

Take In a Partner

In my opinion this should be a very last resort. I know that many real estate agents and investors advise the partnership approach to raising capital. In my own experience, however, I've found that taking in a partner means adding a headache.

Invariably your ideas and expectations are going to differ from your partner's, and this can lead to hurt feelings, tension, or even lawsuits. It can all be avoided by not having partners.

On the other hand, having now stated my own preference, if you are still determined to move ahead with a partnership, there are two types that have become very popular in recent years.

Syndication

"Syndication" is a term commonly used in real estate to describe a "limited partnership." In a typical limited partnership, you put up your expertise and others put up the money. The idea is that if you want to raise $30,000, it's a lot easier to find ten people willing to put up $3000 apiece than to find one willing to risk the whole $30,000. Syndication is a way of bringing partners into a real estate deal.

In a limited-partnership syndication there are typically two different types of partner. There is the general partner (you) who is responsible for everything that happens (including foreclosure and personal injury lawsuits). Then there is the "limited" partner who invests the money and hopes to get part of the profit but who has very limited exposure and liability.

For friends and relatives who want to invest, this can be an excellent capital-raising device.

It must be understood, however, that a limited-partnership syndication is a legal device. It is regulated by the state you are in and, in some cases, by the Securities and Exchange Commission. Unless you have had great experience with it, you should *not* attempt to create it yourself. Rather, it's something that requires the services of an attorney to set up.

Equity Sharing

This is a method of splitting up the parts of an investment between the needs of two (or more) people. Typically, one person finds the deal and handles the cash flow (collects rents and makes payments) and the other person has the cash but doesn't want to bother getting his or her hands dirty playing around with the property.

The two buy a bargain property together, one contributing cash, the other expertise, and later split the profits. Sometimes it works out quite well.

The essence of equity sharing is the agreement between the partners. It must specify who is to put up what and how the profits are to be divided later. It should also set down the procedure for handling any unforeseen problems that might arise.

Unfortunately, most attorneys simply don't have the occasion to work with equity-sharing agreements. Thus, randomly walking into an attorney's office and asking him or her to create an equity-sharing agreement could be costly and may produce spotty results.

To get such an agreement, you need to find an attorney who specializes in real estate and who handles equity-sharing agreements on a regular basis. Such an attorney can whip one together to fit your needs in a very short time and, hopefully, at a very reduced cost.

The Bottom Line

These then are some of your options when you need to raise cash. There are, of course, many more. In fact, there are entire books largely devoted to just this subject.

The important thing to remember is that if you really need to raise cash for a terrific deal, then in most cases you'll find the money. If the deal is really good, you may have to tell someone else about it (such as a friend or relative), but one way or another you'll come up with the dough. People like you won't let a really terrific opportunity for profit slip through their fingers without a good fight. It's better, of course, if you're prepared in advance and don't have to give away the gravy in the transaction just to be able to put it together.

The Priority of Mortgages

It's important to know the priority of mortgages involved in foreclosure, particularly when bidding at a foreclosure auction (see Chapter 5). Here, briefly, are the rules:

1. The mortgage recorded first has first priority.
2. Tax liens come before any mortgages.
3. Any mortgage can foreclose (first, second, third, etc.), but such foreclosure will not affect superior (lower number) mortgages.

The best way to be sure that we're clear on this is to take an example. Tracy's house has three mortgages on it:

Third mortgage	$10,000
Second mortgage	$20,000
First mortgage	$70,000

Case 1: The first mortgage forecloses. Tracy's house brings $100,000 at the sale.

In this case the loan with the highest priority (the first for $70,000) gets paid off with the first money. Then the loan with the next priority (the second for $20,000) gets paid off. Finally, the loan with the least priority (the third for $10,000) gets paid off. There's no money left, so the owner-borrower gets nothing.

Case 2: As before, the first mortgage forecloses. Tracy's house brings $75,000 at the sale.

Here the loan with the highest priority (the first for $70,000) still gets paid with the first money. Then the loan with the next priority (the second for $20,000) gets paid. However, there is only $5000 left after paying off the first; therefore, the second only gets $5000, despite the fact that the mortgage amount is for $20,000. Since there's no money left after this, the holder of the third gets nothing.

Case 3: The third mortgage forecloses; the first and second are current. The sale brings $10,000. Here the holder of the third mortgage gets the whole $10,000. The first and second mortgages, which were current, are unaffected. The successful buyer now has title to a piece of property with existing first and second mortgages on it. True, this buyer paid $10,000; however, there are already $90,000 of mortgages still on it.

Index

About the Author

Robert Irwin is one of the best-known authors in real estate. He has been a successful California real estate broker for over 20 years, acting as a consultant to other brokers, lenders, investors, and home buyers. He has written and edited nearly a dozen important books on real estate for McGraw-Hill, including *The McGraw-Hill Real Estate Handbook* (1984), *Computerizing Your Real Estate Office* (1985), and *The New Mortgage Game* (1982). His own bargain hunting has netted him many valuable properties.